Jared,
Thank you.
Succeed w/ purpose.
God Bless!
J

SUCCEEDING ON PURPOSE

Strategizing Your Success Through Finding and Living Your Purpose

DR. TONY DANIEL

WESTBOW
PRESS®
A DIVISION OF THOMAS NELSON
& ZONDERVAN

Copyright © 2020 Dr. Tony Daniel.

All rights reserved. No part of this book may be used or reproduced by any means, graphic, electronic, or mechanical, including photocopying, recording, taping or by any information storage retrieval system without the written permission of the author except in the case of brief quotations embodied in critical articles and reviews.

This book is a work of non-fiction. Unless otherwise noted, the author and the publisher make no explicit guarantees as to the accuracy of the information contained in this book and in some cases, names of people and places have been altered to protect their privacy.

WestBow Press books may be ordered through booksellers or by contacting:

WestBow Press
A Division of Thomas Nelson & Zondervan
1663 Liberty Drive
Bloomington, IN 47403
www.westbowpress.com
1 (866) 928-1240

Because of the dynamic nature of the Internet, any web addresses or links contained in this book may have changed since publication and may no longer be valid. The views expressed in this work are solely those of the author and do not necessarily reflect the views of the publisher, and the publisher hereby disclaims any responsibility for them.

Any people depicted in stock imagery provided by Getty Images are models, and such images are being used for illustrative purposes only. Certain stock imagery © Getty Images.

ISBN: 978-1-9736-9238-6 (sc)
ISBN: 978-1-9736-9239-3 (hc)
ISBN: 978-1-9736-9237-9 (e)

Library of Congress Control Number: 2020910437

Print information available on the last page.

WestBow Press rev. date: 06/12/2020

Contents

Acknowledgments vii
Preface ix

Chapter 1   The Concept of Purpose 1
Chapter 2   A Different World 22
Chapter 3   It's Closer Than You Think 43
Chapter 4   The Real You 52
Chapter 5   Commit to the Cause 69
Chapter 6   The Battle with Adversity 82
Chapter 7   Executing the Plan 94
Chapter 8   Tearing Down the Walls 117

Epilogue 141
Notes 145

Acknowledgments

Dedicated to my loving wife, Beverly, who has supported me through the difficult times when my dreams seemed so far away. She reminded me of my potential and encouraged me throughout this process. Also, to my mother, Ruth, who always taught me to make my dreams possible through hard work. She always told me that I could accomplish anything I decided upon, as long as I was willing to pay the price. Although she is not here to see the fruition, she was the first to believe in me. To all those who reviewed the text and provided valuable feedback, thank you for your effort and honesty. To my colleagues at WestBow Press for all of the help during this journey, thank you for your patience and care.

Preface

As I entered midlife, crashing into the head-spin of evaluating where I had been, my accomplishments, and the relationships I had gained and sacrificed, I looked at the world around me and questioned not only my existence but also my significance to it. I had spent many years drudging through the daily activities to support my family, raise my children to be good citizens, and conform to the routine expectations that come along with life. Up to that point, I had spent my lifetime making a living, but I realized that I had failed to make a life, or at least live it. It was time for a change, but I had no idea where to begin.

During an outing with a friend, I related this feeling of longing for more and that I was wondering what was happening to me. I had a great life, great friends, and a great career, but I needed more—or at least something that I could tell others about who I am and why I exist. Two weeks later, my friend gave me a book. It was about the realization that there are two halves to life; the first is about working and attaining, while the second is about significance and realizing that there is one thing as the most important. As I read the book, it was as if the author had sat down and talked with me about my thinking and emotions. I couldn't put the book down and finished reading it in two days. Now I knew what I had been missing and what God was trying to tell me. I had been living to survive instead of living with purpose. Now the work began to learn more about me, my purpose, my strengths, my value to others, and how I could provide these to the world.

My research on the topic opened a new world of understanding. I learned how purpose had driven so many individuals to focus their energies toward specific outcomes. I learned that my life was already an expression of my purpose, whether it operated consciously or subconsciously. I learned how servanthood was a great phenomenon that drove these individuals to seek the good of others before themselves. I learned how understanding purpose directed a bridled passion within these individuals, driving them to act and execute their purpose, and the results it brought to others. I learned that everyone was unique and used their innate talents and gifts to help others. I read how these individuals, many who had experienced and overcome high obstacles, were, at one time, facing the same crossroad where I found myself: they had wondered, sought, found, realized, and were living their purpose.

This was an epiphany for me. I learned that these individuals, many who had accomplished great things, were ordinary individuals who found their place in the world. The common denominator was that they understood that the concept of purpose alone was not enough. However, when it was used to fuel passion, the result was a focused set of actions that brought extraordinary results. They understood the value they brought to the world around them and sought specific opportunities to provide it each day. They understood that commitment was a necessary ingredient to help sustain them through the struggles encountered along their way. I found that their clarity of who they were helped them see personal walls that were blocking their progress, and they found specific ways to tear them down. As you read this book, think about and internalize the concepts. Make them personal and create a workable set of goals and strategies to accomplish them. Your purpose is not some mythical phenomenon that you cannot reach and enjoy. It is not something that happens to just a few individuals. It is within your reach. Many books have been written about accomplishing your dreams. Yet, within the chapters of this book, you will learn a concrete strategy to find your purpose and put it into action. Once you find it, a passion will arise that will provide the fuel to drive you every day to seek out the resources needed for a life of significance. It will breed conviction and turn mediocrity into excellence. It will harness a tone of life force energy and will become contagious to those around you. Realizing, pursuing, and living your purpose will set your life in motion.

Your destiny is waiting. Your purpose will direct you; your passion will fuel you; your performance will secure you.

Chapter 1

The Concept of Purpose

It concerns us to know the purposes we seek in life, for then, like archers aiming at a definite mark, we shall be more likely to attain what we want.

—Aristotle

In a quiet moment during the cattle drive in the movie *City Slickers*, Curly opened up to Mitch and told him about his most unforgettable memory. It was the day he saw the most beautiful woman ever. It was seared in his heart and soul. She was a redhead whose hair, while pinning clothes on a line, glistened in the sun. He instantly fell in love. When Mitch asked him what happened, Curly said, "Nothing. That was it."

When asked why, Curly replied, "I figured it wouldn't ever get any better than that."

Mitch pushed the moment and questioned Curly about how he knew that and if he ever wondered what would have happened. Curly just looked at him and asked, "Do you know what the secret to life is?"

Feeling confused, Mitch replied, "What?"

Curly held up one finger.

Mitch, to lighten the moment, asked, "What, your finger?"

Curly replied, "It's one thing."

Mitch asked, "What's the one thing?"

Curly stopped the horse, looked intensely at Mitch, and replied, "That's what you have to figure out."[1]

Mitch and his friends had left the big city and traveled to the open country to experience a cattle drive, hoping that, by some chance, they could find meaning in their lives. Later, Mitch Robbins would revisit Curly's words as he risked his life to save a calf he had befriended. He realized he had been searching for meaning in things instead of within himself.

The Foundations of Purpose

Purpose is a term that can be difficult to define. It can mean different things to different people. Many authors refer to it as your destiny. However, destiny is a final destination or outcome. To whatever definition you ascribe, the concept remains the same—purpose is the most essential part of you. It is your deepest dimension, settled at your inner core, and waiting to be fed by you. Your purpose is your contribution to the world around you. The realization that you were created for a specific purpose is sobering, and seeking it will set your life in motion and help you discover new perspectives. Your purpose will create direction and harness a life force energy that will help guide you. It's not about optimism. It's not about emotions. It's about finding and pursuing *the call*. Your purpose will fulfill your destiny—but only if you create a plan filled with goals and do the steps to reach each one.

As I take you through the process of finding and living your purpose, you need a point of origin to help provide a foundational perspective. You will read many times that your purpose is very close to you. Finding your purpose is a process, and grasping the concept of purpose requires you to think differently. To begin your journey, I've listed five questions for you to answer, or at least begin pondering, that will help you start the cognitive processes of narrowing your focus to areas where your purpose may exist. Although not inclusive, they will provide you with a place to begin. At the end of this chapter, you can write down your answers. Referring back to them as you read the other chapters will help you focus on the reality of your purpose and eliminate areas you are not suited for.

The other sections in this chapter are not necessarily application based but will help you understand what purpose does and does not entail. You will learn that the inner voice is an intricate part of guidance. It is not the only mechanism of decision-making but is a part of the process. You will read about the differences in combining success and significance as part of pursuing and applying your purpose. The courage to chase your dreams and maintaining the passion of the pursuit are critical components that will keep you going when nothing seems to go right or when you face roadblocks.

Five Important Questions

1. What are some areas and (or) activities that enthrall you?
   The word *enthrall* means to leave spellbound or in awe. What topics or areas keep your attention so much that you can't seem to get enough information? Steve Jobs stated,

"The only way to do great work is to love what you do. If you haven't found it yet, keep looking. Don't settle." One way to find this is to be aware of things or areas that bring you joy when either thinking about them, doing them, or both. If you're fortunate enough, you can relate to Tiger Woods, a professional golfer, who stated, "I get to play golf for a living. What more can you ask for—getting paid for doing what you love?"

2. If money were no object, what would you do for free?

An old Chinese proverb says, "Find something you love to do, and you'll never have to work a day in your life." When you love what you do, you don't see it as work. You don't mind getting out of bed and doing it because you have an understanding of why you do it. After graduating high school, my youngest son had no idea what he wanted to do. He really wasn't an academic, so college was probably not a good choice. He had become interested in welding, so he attended a local technical college. However, he soon realized that welding wasn't something he wanted to pursue. I knew that he had to find his place, so I told him to go to work for a couple of years, and maybe something would emerge as an interest. During the next four years, he worked a regular job but also became interested in working on automobiles, especially foreign ones. Seeing his passion, I suggested he look into a program at the local technical college he had attended four years prior. He found that he could attend and receive certifications in the field of automotive technology. While attending, he went to work in a local automotive shop as an apprentice. He has told me on more than one occasion that it was a life-changing time and he never feels like he is at work because of how much he loves what he does each day.

3. What is your inspiration or motivation to get out of bed?

Jerry Lewis, actor and philanthropist, stated, "That never stops. That's what drives you—the joy and excitement of doing what you love." Andy Grammer, American singer and songwriter, said, "As a musician, you just want to be able to do what you love." Fully understanding why you do what you do will fuel your passion. This passion drives you to look for opportunities to express your passion. It burns deep inside of you. This burning is motivation that guides how you think and behave. The more you listen to it, the closer you come to your purpose.

4. What activities do you participate in where you hardly recognize the passing time?

I've loved baseball since I was old enough to hold a ball and put on a glove. I learned to catch by throwing a tennis ball against the house and fielding it as it bounced back. Just before my eighth birthday, we moved from a mill village in southwest Atlanta to a subdivision in the Stone Mountain, Georgia, community. It was a great neighborhood with a lot of children my age. I instantly gained a friend named Ronnie, who lived across the street. He also loved baseball. We had no place to play baseball in the neighborhood, so we would play in the street. The problems this caused were obvious: we would hit cars and, occasionally, a glass in a house. We were always interrupted by cars. Of course, we had to stop playing until the car passed.

Ronnie's dad worked for an excavation company and drove large earth-moving equipment. There was a huge vacant field at the end of the street that was littered with logs, rocks, and other debris. Understanding our problem and having to listen to complaints from local neighbors, Ronnie's dad brought home a dozier and graded the field. We now had a baseball field where we could spend hours playing. There were countless times I would look up and see my mom standing there, motioning for me to come home. She would remind me that I had been there all day. The time passed so fast. I was reminded of these times when *The Sandlot* was released in 1993. The group of neighborhood kids in the movie had passion that was exhibited by meeting at a sandlot ballfield to play baseball; they, too, were oblivious to the amount of time spent there. Billy Porter, American Broadway performer, stated, "When you're doing what you love, it's not exhausting at all, actually. It's completely empowering and exhilarating." What are activities that you do that keep you so interested you lose track of time? Pay close attention to them and write them down. These are a very important part of the process of clarifying your purpose.

5. What topics do you think about when alone?

This could also relate to the first one. If you could make a list of the ideas that you think about most often, what would you include? The difference here is the thought process of topics. What topics interests you the most? What do you find yourself thinking about at different times throughout the day? Swami Vivekananda, a nineteenth-century Hindu monk, said, "Take up one idea. Make that one idea your life—think of it, dream of it, live on that idea. Let the brain muscles, nerves, every part of your body, be full of that idea, and just leave every other idea alone. This is the way to success." As you sit alone, during your quiet time, what do you think about? Do specific topics keep recurring to you? Pay close attention to these and write them down.

As you work through your list, pay close attention to patterns that emerge. You should see some similarities among the items on the list, which you can use as a guide throughout the rest of the chapters. Refer back to the list as you read and work through the exercises. It's not the individual items that are important but the patterns that emerge.

The Inner Voice

The sense of purpose is something that cannot be heard or seen, yet it provides a yearning that sometimes you can't understand. It is your *inner self* speaking to you and offering guidance. It lives in the deeper flow of your life, the meaning underlying the events. It cannot be found in the events themselves or what you can see with the natural eye but comes from the inside and manifests itself outwardly.

Research about leadership indicates that one of the common

attributes of good leaders is the strength of intuition, that *gut feeling* that is difficult to recognize and impossible to measure. Effective leaders pay close attention to intuition and include it in the mix of decision-making. Over the years, I've ignored it more than once and paid the price. This voice of intuition roars insight into your life, which provides you with knowledge about something without you understanding why. Your inner voice is the GPS of your journey and is relentless in pursuing you. It pushes you and corrects you when you deviate from the course. It knows who you are. It knows more about you than you know about yourself. It knows what value you bring to the world. It knows for what purpose you were created and continues to cry out within you, pushing you to seek it out. This voice knows no limitations and cannot be contained by status, career, houses, cars, or other possessions.

As you reflect over the years, you are likely to recollect many experiences or situations that seemed to be coincidental. Although separate events, you may see them now as a pattern. These situations are what the psychologist Carl Yung termed *synchronicity*—those coincidences that happen that are just a little too coincidental. Many may seem to have occurred out of place or for no reason. You can't explain why they happened. This nagging feeling keeps pushing and pursuing. Stop and listen, for it holds wisdom for your journey of purpose.

Stephen Covey, professor and author, described the inner voice as a *unique personal significance*, a combination of need, conscience, passion, and talent.[2] There again, because your purpose is already there, waiting on you to discover it, this voice knows when you are on the right path. A cycle develops. When you make a right decision, it propels you and fuels the passion for serving that purpose. When you don't make the right decision, it checks you. In return, the passion energizes a desire to seek its meaning and act accordingly. You will naturally seek out things and situations to help fulfill it. Your talents and strengths, which will be discussed later, provide you with the mechanism to locate and focus your energy toward a specific path.

Purpose Defines Success

Success is difficult to define. It means different things to different people and is measured in a variety of ways. Society at large views success in terms of the amount of your income, size of your house, what type of car you drive, or the type of job or profession you have. We observe that, while on the surface, individuals place a high value on things, having these items does not create happiness or qualify as success. Helen Keller stated, "Many people have a wrong idea of what constitutes true happiness. It is not obtained through self-gratification, but through fidelity to a worthy purpose." Suicide rates among celebrities remain high—a group who, based on society's terms, should be the happiest of all individuals. Yet there is a deep longing that cannot be satisfied by possessions that truly do not define them. Instead of searching, finding, and living that *one thing*, most live based on the expectations of others, never fully realizing the power at their fingertips through pursuing, finding, and living their purpose with passion. Viktor Frankl, an Austrian neurologist, psychiatrist, and Holocaust survivor, pointed out, "People today have the means to live, but no meaning to live for."[3]

Searching for and finding your purpose is a very important part of true success. You have a purpose—something that charts you toward your destiny. It combines all the abilities, talents, desires, and skills needed to produce a specified outcome. Richard Leider, founder of Inventure—The Purpose Company, believed "Purpose is the reason a person is born. From birth to death, each of us is on a quest to discover that reason. Many never do. Yet, our world is incomplete until each one of us discovers our purpose."[4] One problem is that most people, due to living through the expectations of others, do not think this way and never realize that finding that purpose offers endless opportunities. Thomas Merton wrote that all you really need is already in your life. He called it the *hidden wholeness.* Leider explained it a little differently: "Purpose is that deepest dimension within us—our central core or essence—where we have a profound sense of who we are, where we came from, and where we're going. Purpose is the quality around which we choose to shape our lives. Purpose is a source of energy and direction."[5]

Instead of focusing outward to find your place in the world based on the expectations of others, search inward. It is a longing, a hollow place located within you that you desire to fill in the core of your soul. It is the most essential part of you waiting to be fed, the discovering of what's true about you rather than overlaying someone else's truth on you or injecting someone else's goals onto your personality. Its valuable revelation comes only through diligent searching of your inner self. It's what makes you tick, and receiving a spark will ignite a flame of passion. You will find it among your deepest desires, your aspirations, and among those things you would do even if you were never paid.

You experience life through your emotions, not just your intellect. Your purpose is vibrantly aware and in touch with your emotional core. The more you are connected to that core, the more sense of purpose you feel. You will experience a tremendous amount of energy protruding outwardly instead of reacting to outward circumstances.

Success is a process and something that does not occur in one day. It can take years of trial and error, observing one's self, and defining the meaning of life. Those who find it are those who have persevered through hardships, mistakes, and sacrifice. Those who find it early represent a small percentage. The process of selecting a goal, determining a course of action that aligns with that goal, establishing a systematic plan to accomplish it, and then pursuing it demands stamina, determination, and commitment. This becomes difficult to accept and implement in our current society of technological advancement where information is literally at our fingertips. Once your purpose is clear, a natural passion will arise and create a desire within you that will push you daily. The quest brings a reward that you are using your gifts and strengths in the pursuit of what you were created to do and making a contribution that brings contentment.

Dr. Tony Daniel

Purpose Transforms Success into Significance

Several years ago, I heard the phrase *unique personal significance*. At first, I found it to be very abstract. However, the more I thought about it, the more interested I became. I wondered how to pursue it—and how would I know if I reached it? The term *unique* is defined by *Merriam-Webster* as *being the only one, being without a like or equal, distinctively characteristic, and unusual*. It is not a generic term or a fit-all perspective. It is not a slang term to be thrown around in consulting or self-help circles. It is a specific attribute that you have been given. However, being unique is only the first word. The next two provide the action component.

Although your purpose is your reason for existence, it is rarely to serve you alone. Personal significance reaches for a higher purpose to fulfill the needs of others. It is more than success. The concept of significance can be recognized through an old Cherokee saying, "When you were born, you cried and the world rejoiced; live your life in such a way when you die, the world cries and you rejoice." The entertainer Danny Thomas stated, "All of us are born for a reason, but all of us don't discover why. Success in life has nothing to do with your gain in life or what you accomplish for yourself. It's about what you do for others." Actress Audrey Hepburn stated, "Are you bored with life? Then throw yourself into some work you believe in with all your heart. Live for it, die for it, and you will find happiness that you thought could never be yours." W. E. Gladstone stated, "Never forget that the purpose for which a man lives is the improvement of the man himself, so that he may go out of this world having, in his great sphere or his small one, done some little good for his fellow creatures and labored a little to diminish the sin and sorrow that are in the world."

These sayings drive home the higher plane of significance above success. It's a delicate and dangerous zone. Success to many is about getting as much stuff as possible. Significance is about getting as much success as possible without getting captured by it. Significance is about making the world a better place for all. It is about putting others before yourself. Hans Selye, a microbiologist from Canada, coined the phrase *altruistic egoism.* He explained it as nothing more than the biblical truth that helping others helps you. He learned that those who earn the goodwill of their neighbor are dramatically better off psychologically and physiologically than those who are looked upon as selfish and greedy. Finding and living through a purpose of significance pushes you and unlocks the door to your larger self.

I was born to older parents, ages fifty-one and forty-five. I remember their stories of the Roaring Twenties, the Great Depression, losing a child at birth, World War II, and the struggles they faced. They were members of a distinct generation that held a great amount of respect for authority and the values on which America were founded. Most in this generation worked only one to two places throughout a career and were very loyal to the organization through good times and bad.

Through my years of research, I asked members of my parents' generation how they would live their life differently if they had the chance. Although there were many personal examples, the responses seemed to be grouped into three categories. First, they would be more reflective. In other words, they would be more in tune with their environment. They would stop more often and gauge their success to some form of goal system. Second, they would be more courageous. They would take more risks and be less afraid of change. Finally, most said they would work harder to understand themselves better and live with purpose.

Purpose Expands Your Boundaries

Finding your purpose and living it each day provides a variety of benefits, which I will discuss throughout the remainder of this book. However, purpose living follows the realization that each of us is born for a specific reason. The sad part is that so many never discover why. President Calvin Coolidge stated, "No enterprise can exist for itself alone. It ministers to some great need, it performs some great service, not for itself, but for others; or failing therein it ceases to be profitable and ceases to exist." You are not here to merely make a living. Years earlier, President Woodrow Wilson stated, "You are here in order to enable the world to live more amply, with greater vision, with a finer spirit of home and achievement. You are here to enrich the world, and you impoverish yourself if you forget the errand." This is a great explanation of the difference between success, which is internally focused, and significance, which is externally focused. Such significance is found through a calling, not a job.

Branding Your Purpose

Are you recognized by your purpose? What you do has little to do with who you are. However, who you are has everything to do with what you do. Your actions define you and speak volumes about your priorities. Your work is a portrait of yourself. It is your brand. When people hear your name, they will associate you with your purpose. You will assume a new identity based on the unique characteristics of the brand. Author and former professor at the University of Utah, Stephen Covey, related that whatever is at the center of your life will be the source of your security, guidance, wisdom, and power.[6] You assume an identity to friends, coworkers, and social networks who know you by what you do. Is what you do an indication of who you really are? As Curly described, you must find that *one thing*. Purpose is not multifunctional. Regardless of your position in life, once you have identified your one thing, you will experience clarity and freedom in life.

The Passion of Pursuit

Greek philosopher Socrates often held sessions with his protégés on topics of deep thinking. During a session on the power of passion, one of his students asked about the easiest path to knowledge. To make his point, Socrates invited the student over to a barrel of water. He then took the student by the head and pushed his head under the water. The young student began thrashing violently, needing air. Finally, Socrates pulled the student's head out of the water, and as the boy gasped for air, Socrates asked him, "When you were under the water, what was the one thing you wanted more than anything else?"

"I wanted air!" yelled the student.

Socrates replied, "When you want knowledge and understanding as badly as you wanted air, you won't have to ask anyone to give it to you."

Although seeking, realizing, and pursuing your purpose is the first step in success, it is only part of the process. The road is never easy, filled with disappointments and detours. For this reason, many have sought for purpose but failed to channel the passion to pursue it. Passion without action is merely a desire, which has little or no value to others. However, once you become fully aware of your purpose and have set your heart on seeking it daily, a passion within you is fueled, an internal motivation that keeps you moving even when there is no tangible reward in sight. It's a fire that burns despite others' attempt to extinguish it. It is often criticized because it may sometimes be viewed as undisciplined, an overly emotional state. However, when passion is fueled by purpose, it becomes a bridled, clear, and unstoppable force that creates enough momentum to cut through fear and exhaustion and move forward in the face of criticism and adversity. Kathleen Bader, Business Group president at DOW Chemical explained that unless you work according to your passion and your values, you have no hope of living authentically. Because of your clear sense of purpose, your passion becomes directed toward fulfillment instead of undirected emotion.

The Search Demands Courage

Walt Disney stated, "All of our dreams can come true, if we have the courage to pursue them." Many dream about a better life and seek a variety of things to help fulfil the longing. However, the pursuit requires an enormous amount of courage. It demands taking risks that are outside of your comfort zone. You must work to accumulate a variety of perspectives in your interpretation of the world, moving you to question every paradigm of your life and justify your thinking, motives, and behavior. There will always be those who sit on the sideline and continually critique those on the field. These lack the courage to get out of the stands and enter the game. Those who attempt to hold you back, due to misunderstanding the power of purpose, fear, or some other reason, attempt to keep you on the sideline with them where it's comfortable. They want to excel but, becoming derailed by their own doubt, criticize those who see a need, make the preparation, gather the courage, and then implement a plan. Purpose demands that you stretch beyond average or the status quo. You can't reach for it and remain mediocre at the same time. These two are incompatible.

Reaching beyond your comfort zone can have a lasting impact on you and inspire others. In a story told by Girolamo Benzoni, in his book *History of the New World*, he related a story. Although the accuracy may be questionable, the story is appropriate here. It is about Christopher Columbus, who, while at a party with Spanish nobles, was approached by a group of men who minimized his discovery of the New World as a matter of luck and time, believing that eventually another of the great men in Spain would have made the journey. Columbus, calling for a raw egg, placed it on the table and challenged all, by wager, to make it stand upright on its end. After all of them tried and none succeeded, Columbus took the egg, tapped it on the table, flattening one end, and stood it upright. One of the men cried, "Any of us could have done that!" Columbus responded, "Yes, if you had only known how. And once I showed you the way to the New World, nothing was easier than to follow it."[7]

There are those who dream and lack the courage to pursue. Yet there are those who have visualized things that do not yet exist, gathered the courage, fed the passion, created a plan, and then disciplined themselves to stay the course to fruition. Such courage is exhibited in the discipline of execution. General George S. Patton, a renowned World War II leader who led the offensive across North Africa and parts of Europe, told his commanders, "There's one thing I want you to remember. I don't want to get any messages saying we are holding our position. Holding a position is for cowards. We are advancing constantly."

The difference in success and failure lies among those intended actions to fulfill a dream. Decisions and desires may be honorable but become empty without action. Passion creates commitment that allows obstacles to be seen as targets. Purpose sets the course, passion provides the fuel, and action provides the evidence. None of these are possible without courage—the willingness to step outside of your comfort zone and toward something that may seem so crazy to you and others, yet knowing that you are being pulled to fulfill it. Purpose is the key to passion. Passion is the key to persistence. The courage and persistence to endure obstacles and build on them is the key to performance. The absence of one leaves a gap in the process. The result is an overcompensation, which results in an unauthentic inward purpose and an outward exhibition of falsehood.

Your purpose is closer than you think. You already possess the strengths to pursue and achieve it. It lies within you now and is ready to be exposed. Once you find it, protect it, nurture it, and feed it with passion. Let this passion lead you to action and experience a higher level of self-worth, success, and significance. It is near yet elusive. Two main components of finding your purpose, listening and searching, will provide you with a starting point.

Five Questions

This exercise will help you begin to narrow your focus and identify areas where your purpose may lie. Below, you will find the five questions regarding the foundation of purpose. Think about each one and write down your thoughts. Be creative and let your mind wander. You will refer to and revise the list as you read the remaining chapters.

1. What are some areas/activities that enthrall you?

2. If money was no object, what would you do for free?

3. What is your inspiration or motivation to get out of bed each morning?

4. What activities do you participate in where you hardly recognize the passing of time?

5. What topics to you think about during your quiet time?

Chapter 2

A Different World

> To the man who only has a hammer in the toolkit,
> every problem looks like a nail.
> —Abraham Maslow, American psychologist

The thought of change is unsettling to most people. In a later chapter, I discuss the tearing down of walls that handicap you from executing your purpose. Change is difficult in the best set of circumstances. However, changing the way you think is most difficult. Humans are creatures of habit. We learn specific ways of doing things, most without understanding why, and do them repeatedly with ease. This chapter is about clarity, seeing the world with a different set of eyes and the freedom it brings in the pursuit of your purpose. The first step is to realize that how we see the world may be hampering our ability to see clearly. It's expedient to understand the power of paradigms and to question their validity in your life.

The Power of Paradigms

Have you ever wondered why two people interpret a single event two different ways? Each holds a belief that their interpretation is true. This is an example of the power of paradigms. A paradigm is defined as a philosophical or theoretical framework of any kind. Paradigms are very powerful patterns of thinking that have an impact on your behavior and can obstruct your path to fulfilling your purpose. You learn paradigms from a variety of institutions in your life, including parents, teachers, church, peers, workplace, and so on. You never question them because you assume they are correct or the best way of doing something. You may even arrange your life around them and attempt to justify them when challenged. You interpret the world and filter information through these powerful paradigms. Information that disagrees with your paradigm is judged to be inappropriate or false and is therefore discarded.

Here, the strength of paradigms must be examined. They are not patterns of behavior but patterns of thinking that drive your interpretation of the world around you. You formulate perspectives about your world and therefore behave based on them. Why is this important? In looking at your overall context in life, you project the qualities of your paradigms onto yourself. This projection becomes your role in reality. It is the core of your belief system. You act it out through interactions with others. Therefore, to change the way you act, you must change the way you think. Don't make the mistake of assuming you can change who you are to find your purpose. Your purpose will change you and your way of thinking. Clarity of your purpose will create new boundaries that set you up to be realized through accomplishment. But how do you do this?

I was raised in Georgia and have the southern accent that never leaves those around me wondering where I'm from. A few years ago, I was in Boston for a conference. As I walked from my hotel to the conference center, I saw this professionally dressed female approaching. We arrived at the front door at the same time, so I politely opened the door. I didn't speak but gave a slight nod of my head, indicating that I was waiting on her to enter. She entered, and I followed. After four of five steps, she stopped, turned, and looked at me intently. I stopped and immediately wondered what I had done. I just stood there. She put her hands on her hips and said, "You're from the South, aren't you?"

Being confused, I looked her and wondered how she knew this, or at least why she would ask. At this point, I had not spoken. Feeling confused, I replied, "I am, but how did you know?"

She smiled and stated, "I didn't but presumed because you held the door for me. Guys up here don't hold the door for women." I'm not sure if she had ever been to the South, but she obviously held the paradigm of a *southern gentleman*. I told her that holding a door for others, especially females, was a value my mother taught me at a young age. I still do it today.

You accept your paradigms as truths and form your behavior around them. You never question why you think and therefore behave a certain way. You then project your interpretation onto others. Without an awareness of the power these paradigms have on your thinking and behavior, change in any form becomes very difficult. Many search for ways to adapt their environment to their paradigms instead of recognizing and evaluating them as part of the problem.

Seeking such clarity will demand that you question your paradigms. Doing so will carry you through a lot of self-searching, questioning, and evaluating. Through this process, you will experiment through much trial and error. However, you will find something that relates to your purpose and may be a small piece of a larger puzzle. It is here that you begin to question the world around you and your motives, perspectives, existence, and other components of your life. You will open new avenues of thinking that will bleed over into every part of your life. You will gain understanding about why your interest is drawn to certain things and not others. It will allow you to evaluate those paradigms to reality. Those that have no basis in reality, or just because that's the way you've always done it, can be eliminated or changed. It will illuminate your deepest life intentions to empower you to move with greater focus every day of your life, which will provide an intense awareness of your surroundings and the signs that are presented. This new intensity of awareness creates an atmosphere of least work, which sounds contradictory to what you've read thus far. However, you now become fine-tuned into the work that is natural to you. That moment could come at any time. It could be instantaneous or through a series of events, as in Gretta's life.

Gretta's Journey

Gretta was born and raised in western Kentucky by two loving parents. Her dad was an x-ray technician with a steel company. Her mother worked with the Kentucky Inspection Bureau, a fire insurance rating agency. She had a normal childhood and enjoyed many social activities during her years of high school. After graduation, she attended Western Kentucky University but left before graduation. She married and began a family. She found a job in a local insurance agency that was a subsidiary of a national company. Her position gave her the opportunity to network with leaders of other companies throughout the country.

After the death of Gretta's husband and her son's high school graduation, she accepted a position at a large insurance company in Pennsylvania as the chief operating officer. By this time, Gretta was enjoying a six-figure income and the benefits of her success. Gretta worked hard and continued to advance in her chosen field. She was recruited for a COO position at a large insurance company in Georgia, which she accepted. Her office was one of grandeur. The walls were decorated with expensive paintings by famous artists of the past, most costing more than her annual salary. Her office furniture was very elegant and expensive. Her desk was massive in size, with unmatched detailed woodwork.

However, Gretta felt something was missing. She felt that there had to be more and that she may not, after all of her success, be really making a difference. She began volunteering at a local shelter for abused and neglected children who were placed there by the courts or social service agencies. Some were short-term, and others were long-term placements. She watched these children accept her love, which was something most had not received from their own parents and relatives. She began to see the world differently and began to feel a satisfaction that had not been there in years. She began to question her motives as she listened to an inner voice she had not heard before. She didn't understand these feelings that she was now experiencing.

Gretta continued her volunteer activities in the evenings and weekends while working at the insurance company during the day. One day, the CEO of the insurance company walked into her office and informed her that the company was being acquired by a larger company in Florida. He assured her that she was a valuable asset to the company. He had spoken with the CEO of the other company, and a position was waiting for her there. At that point, Gretta knew she had a decision to make. She knew she had arrived at a pivotal point in her life and career. The inner voice that she had been hearing was screaming in one ear, while the natural voice of her surroundings was screaming in the other.

She went to the children's home as usual to work and told the staff what had happened and that she had been offered the position in Florida. The next day, Gretta received a call from the chairperson of the board of directors at the children's home, who informed her that the director had resigned. The chairperson then asked her if she would be interested in taking the job. How could she leave a six-figure income, take a serious cut in pay, leave behind the fine art and furniture, and work as a director at a nonprofit children's home? She suddenly found herself experiencing something she had never felt before. Those things, including the salary and the perks, no longer seemed important.

Dr. Tony Daniel

As I sat in her office at the children's home, I looked around and noticed countless hand-drawn pieces of artwork on her walls and door. The home's residents through the years had drawn such pieces of artwork and given them to her with the only thing they had to offer—a grateful heart. I listened as she told a story about each drawing. She related each child's background along with his or her successes and failures. As she spoke, the passion for her work was transparent. As she pointed to one drawing, I was moved as her voice cracked while describing the child's background and failure at the home, followed by the excitement about the story associated with the next one. She described such details with an enormous amount of clarity. Watching and listening, I knew that she had no doubt about her life-changing decision years earlier and that she was where she was supposed to be.[1]

Gretta provides a great example of the meaning and importance of clarity in finding and fulfilling your purpose. Having a clear understanding of who you are, what you are meant to do, and why illuminates details that help you set goals to achieve your purpose. Gaining this clarity directs intentional passion. Any goal contrary to it, even though it could be attained, results in a lack of self-fulfillment and joy. Susan Sontag, American writer, filmmaker, teacher, and political activist, related that she was not looking for her dreams to interpret her life but rather for her life to interpret her dreams. During our interview, Gretta stated, "I was existing and was so busy trying to make a living, it never occurred to me that I was not living at all. My whole perspective of life and world changed in just a few months. I will forever be grateful for the opportunities given me."

Gretta's clarity provided a 180-degree shift in her perspective of the world around her. What was once important became secondary. All of her energy was focused on this new clarity of purpose and fulfillment. She related the feeling of empowerment and freedom that she had experienced. Her life was much more meaningful, and she had rewritten the list of priorities in her life. She no longer faced the dread of getting up and going to work. She knew why she was going to work, which motivated her with energy for a higher calling. As I sat with her, she looked at me, and with a smile on her face, she said, "My life is complete. I can't imagine it could get any better." She had made the transition from working for success to working for significance. She had experienced a significant *paradigm shift*.

Purpose Drives Empowerment

The clarity that results from the realization of purpose will empower you in all contexts of your life. You will choose better inputs, which will result in better outputs. Your decision-making will become more focused and accurate because you now have a gauge to measure each scenario you face. If your context is an inaccurate fit for reality, corrupted by too many false beliefs and incorrect assumptions, then you're unlikely to be able to define a meaningful purpose for your life, no matter what method you use. Remember, your context is your collection of beliefs about reality. In fact, your focus determines your reality.

Although there are a lot of things you could be doing, your defined clarity will guide you toward what you should be doing. A vibrant awareness of your emotional core will provide you with a tremendous amount of energy in your life. This sense of empowerment allows you to mark boundaries. In fact, your purpose will mark them for you. When others attempt to pull you to one side or the other, those boundaries will keep you upright. They will not allow you to be distracted and changed. Because who you are is founded on purpose, you cannot be lured into a falsehood of hope or dreams. The consistency of purpose becomes your guide.

Purpose Reorganizes Your Priorities

Throughout medical school, students are encouraged to choose a field of specialization. Doing so identifies an expertise in a certain area of medicine and identifies a clear map of priority, study, and practice. Defined priorities eliminate the emotional strain of being something to everyone. This is the reason your doctor may refer you to another for a specific area. You are best when you are the expert at your one thing. In business, organizational leaders seek the competitive advantage of their organization in the marketplace. Once they find that one thing, it is marketed and branded. Soon, those who hear the company's name relate it to its competitive advantage. For example, Chick-fil-A, a national restaurant chain that is known for its delicious chicken sandwiches, was started by Truett Cathy in 1946. Customer service is a high priority and a competitive advantage for the company. Each day, this brand is supported throughout more than 2,300 restaurants across America. The words of Mr. Cathy's dream are alive not only inside the stores but also in the communities across the United States. The same is true with your purpose. The clarity of knowing who you are and what you do best, then creating priorities that add value to you and others, unleashes a greater understanding of you along your journey. Again, whatever is at the center of our life will be the source of your security, guidance, wisdom, and power.[2]

As you search, you will gain a greater understanding of what does and doesn't fit. Things that fit can be used to strengthen your core and influence. This is your mainspring—the main goal or vision of accomplishment. In doing so, you project those same qualities onto yourself. This projection becomes your role in reality. You become grounded in your belief system. Those things that do not fit, you cast aside for someone else to take and build upon. Remember, your purpose is a lifelong pursuit. It is a journey, not the final destination. The clarity of priorities provides you with the understanding that adjustments do not alter your outcome, just the process.

Don't look outside of yourself for your priorities. Many rely on the concept of being in the right place at the right time. This is a myth. There have been many who were in the right place at the right time but failed to realize it. Creating priorities, which can be viewed within the concept of preparation, helps you focus on opportunity. When presented, it is more easily recognized, which provides you with the opportunity to seize it.

A great analogy of the concept of priorities is based in

construction. When a builder views the blueprints of a house, he understands that the print includes all sections of the process. But he knows that a good foundation is the priority. He follows the dimensions set within that blueprint and digs the foundation. He understands that if the foundation is not prepared according to the specifications set forth in the blueprint, problems will arise throughout the remainder of the process. It will be impossible for the contractor to follow the blueprint without making some adjustments. Making one adjustment creates the need for more. Soon, his time is spent making adjustments instead of finishing the project. Many ignore the law of priority, and when the details of their lives go awry, they focus only on the outcomes. They fail to realize that they fell short of building the proper priority system. Focusing on the results and not the causes continually wastes time chasing the needed adjustments. There will always be some obstacle, something to be worked through, some unfinished business, time still to be served, a debt to be paid. Therefore, it's necessary to focus on the priorities. What is your one thing? This is your priority, and everything should funnel to it.

As a management development consultant, I am asked by various organizational leaders and managers to devise and implement management development programs. One of the key components of my program is to help managers understand the difference between a problem and the result of one or more problems. Focusing on the result does nothing to alleviate the problem. Therefore, to bring about change, attention must be turned to the root cause of a problem. Scientists, including social scientists, use this methodology when performing research. They use the concept of independent variables, viewed as the cause, and dependent variables, viewed as the results. Manipulating the independent variable creates a change in the dependent variable. The law of priority helps you distinguish between the cause and effect of your efforts. You understand the process of order in formulating a plan based on the priorities.

I was once contacted by a business owner who hired me to do some development with his sales and customer service staff. There had been a 60 percent turnover among his sales and customer service representatives in the last two years. As I talked with my client, he related his thoughts as to the cause of the turnover being low morale and low job satisfaction. I told him that these are the results of deeper issues. I laid out for him a process that I wanted to follow to help clarify the issues. Then we could discuss the results of my assessment, focus on the problem, and create a plan to help him.

After talking with and evaluating the individuals among the positions (I had to create a baseline as to where they were before beginning), it was obvious that the owner had hired individuals not suited for the positions. Using a specific evaluative survey instrument, I evaluated sixteen sales staff and eight customer service reps. Results indicated ten of the first group and six of the second as highly introverted on the scale—something viewed as a weakness for positions where talking to people is a major component of the job. Upon further evaluation, I determined that the business owner had no process in place for identifying individual strengths in the areas needed to succeed as a salesperson and CSR. In fact, his entire hiring process needed to be revised to include processes, including testing instruments, to identify the needed knowledge, skills, and abilities of each applicant to help create a person-to-job fit. My point is that the high turnover was not the problem. Neither was the low morale or job satisfaction. Thinking he was addressing the issues appropriately, the owner had paid training specialists to come in and provide sales technique and customer service training, all to no avail. The problems were much deeper. Once the hiring procedures, including early identification of abilities and strengths through testing, were implemented, turnover was reduced to 4 percent during the next two years. This entire process provided a lot of insight for the business owner. He realized that his priorities were out of order. Once he reorganized his system, the outcomes improved.

Proverbs 1:1–6 relates that you are to find and clarify your purpose and its concepts so that the principles can guide your thinking, decisions, and actions. Knowing who you are and understanding your motives, prejudices, perspectives, and understandings precedes any purpose you may have. The law of priority provides clarity of who you are and what you stand for. It brands your integrity and values. It provides a blueprint for you to use in building your outcome. Anything not directly related can be discarded.

You are the only you. Therefore, your goal should be to build your significance through understanding your uniqueness for that *one thing*. The priority and clarity of this concept provides freedom. Victor Frankl stated, "A man who becomes conscious of the responsibility he bears toward being what affectionately waits for him, or to an unfinished work, will never be able to throw away his life. He knows the *why* for his existence and will be able to bear almost any *how*."

Realize the source or motivating principle behind your purpose—not what you might do to fulfill it. That will come later. The priority is realizing the deeper reasons for you wanting to do it. It helps to eliminate fear and limitation. It allows you to plan your work and work your plan. Priority provides clarity, which sets in motion the other steps in the process. It is here the foundation is laid.

You may ask, "But where do I begin?" As I communicate with leaders and managers at various levels of an organization, I emphasize that the most important component, or priority, of organizational management is the congruency of alignment from the top to the bottom of the organization. The main catalyst for this alignment is the mission statement of the organization. The statement sets the parameter of every activity throughout the organization. This principle of a mission statement is also true for your personal journey.

Personal Mission Statement

One of the main components of strategic management is the power of a mission statement. This statement outlines the reason an organization exists, its value to the marketplace, and the scope of actions that help accomplish it. Every situational opportunity is evaluated against the statement. If it doesn't add value and is not directly related to the mission, it's rejected. The statement provides clarity throughout the workforce as to why everyone comes to work each day and how each job fits into the overall system. It provides a boundary for measurement along the continuum. Every process in every unit must adhere to the accomplishment of the declared mission as it sets in order the activities that support it. Leaders use the mission statement as a guide for strategic decision-making when navigating the industry landscape. Whenever called upon by organizational leaders to help in some area of their organization, the first thing I look for is the mission statement and how visible it is for all employees.

The power of this same process can be reflected in your personal life. You should have a personal mission statement, which you use as a guide to help you evaluate decisions and actions. As a consultant, I've noted to clients that a personal mission statement becomes their *magnetic North Pole and focal point*. By creating the mission statement, you now have the tool to evaluate each opportunity and apply it directly to your purpose.

Whereas an organization's mission statement encompasses the system as a whole, your personal mission statement should be personalized by and for you. It should encompass three distinct areas: what, how, and why. First, what is the main component of your actions? Your statement should clarify the specific market, sector, or cause to which your work should be directed. Second, your statement should provide specific actions of how you will perform your work. It should provide a strategy to the identified what. Third, you should describe an outcome, or the why you do the work. These three areas can be developed separately, however, should be written in one statement that is clear and specific. Your personal mission statement will provide you with guidance as you focus on your purpose.

Below, I have provided my personal mission statement. It provides a clear understanding of the three areas: *what*, *how*, and *why*:

> To develop leaders for the twenty-first-century organization through personal interaction that will empower them to effectively lead others, shape their world, and create value for their organization and communities.

Although I'm approached quite often about helping on different projects, whether it be as a volunteer on a particular board of directors or to assist on a specific task force, I evaluate each through my mission statement. If the task doesn't land within its boundaries, I politely say no. As a result of being consistent, I have been branded in a certain area of expertise. I can now focus my energies, talents, and strengths into what I do best.

In the last section of this book, I discuss the importance of creating a plan to put your purpose to work by letting it fuel your passion to exceed your expectations of performance. Your personal mission statement becomes a vital component of this process. It provides the platform for the evaluation of your outcomes. However, without a clear mission statement, you lack a clear picture of where you are, where you're going, and the ability to accurately measure where you are along the continuum. A few years ago, I was contacted by a broker at a large real estate firm about speaking at their annual awards meeting. I spoke about creating a strategic mentality and linking it to your personal mission statement. I watched as many agents in the company received awards, while others sat and observed. After the meeting, I was approached by one of the agents who was ranked in the lower third of sales for the year; in fact, he was next to last. He was very attentive throughout my presentation and afterward asked me if I could help him. He hired me as a consultant to help him focus his strategy for the coming year. In the early weeks, we met two times per week and addressed a variety of identified issues, including organizing his office (it was a mess). I told him that a messy office is a sign of messy thinking. When he finally cleaned and organized his office, I related to him the principle of a personal mission statement. I told him that it would provide clarity of his work, give him direction, and act as a catalyst for his business. We worked together and settled on a workable mission statement:

> Helping individuals, families, and businesses, through a rewarding experience of effective communication, personalized customer service, and optimal negotiation, realize and achieve their real estate dreams and goals.

Throughout the next year, we concentrated on the importance of focusing on activities instead of commissions. I told him that the commissions would come only after he committed to the activities that fulfilled his mission statement. The next year, he became the top selling agent in the firm and has remained one of the top producers for the last several years. He contributed his success to the mission statement and how it helped him focus his thinking on serving instead of selling. This changed his paradigm, goal preparation, activities, brand, and eventually his outcomes.

During the early stages of the invasion of Afghanistan, the Bush administration was taking some heat from the media on the slow pace of operations and results. In a morning briefing at the White House, President Bush knew that he had to bring his team back into focus and reassure them that they had the right strategy. He outlined that the plan was well conceived, the military was very capable, the cause was just, and, therefore, they should not give in to the second-guessing of others to direct their actions. He stated that they all were going to stay confident and patient, cool and steady. This reassurance brought relief in the room.[3]

Your mission statement provides clarity to sustain you during times of adversity. You will find a calm during times when confusion, being overworked, and stress create uncertainty. Revisiting your personal mission statement renews the clarity for you. It creates a boundary for measurement. You can assess your endeavors based on the what, how, and why of the mission statement. Finding the right path to apply this statement is one that many individuals have searched for throughout time. However, with a clear mission statement, you have the evaluative tool to determine whether your path is correctly leading you to fulfill your purpose. Use the guide to write down the three components of your mission statement. Evaluate each section and refine it. Then put all three together. It should be short, clear, and concise. You'll find a new perspective about you and how you fit into the world. Using your mission statement will open new doors of opportunity and experiences beyond your wildest dreams.

I stated earlier that your purpose is already there; you just have to seek and find it. It's not a mystery but does demand some searching. The search is not easy and can be sobering. However, searching for and finding the innermost parts of you is liberating and the first step in finding your purpose.

Your Personal Mission Statement

A personal mission statement is a guide for decision-making and a boundary for action-oriented activities. It should be short, concise, and clear.

Create your personal mission statement by answering the three questions:

What: This is the main component of your actions. It is directed to a specific segment of people and/or a specific cause. *What* will you be doing?

```
┌─────────────────────────────────────┐
│                                     │
│                                     │
│                                     │
└─────────────────────────────────────┘
```

How: Outline the specifics of *how* you will perform the action you listed in the previous section. *How* will you accomplish the *what*?

```
┌─────────────────────────────────────┐
│                                     │
│                                     │
│                                     │
└─────────────────────────────────────┘
```

Why: Describe the reason for the *what*. It should be specific yet big enough for a greater cause. In other words, why are you doing it?

Personal Mission Statement

Put all components together and refine your statement:

Chapter 3

It's Closer Than You Think

> He is a wise man who wastes no energy on pursuits for which he is not fitted; and he is wiser still who from among the things he can do well, chooses and resolutely follows the best.
> —William Gladstone, nineteenth-century statesman

Through the first two chapters, you were introduced to the concept of purpose, why it is important, and the benefits of working through the process. You've learned about the power of paradigms and how they form ideations about how you interpret your world, the power they have over your thinking and behavior, and how these affect your daily life in the redirection of priorities. Although this seems like a complicated matter and a concept that is difficult to find and reach, it is actually very simple. Let me go ahead and make this statement: *you already possess everything you need to find and fulfill your purpose.* It is not some devoid form you must search for. You don't have to order a book to help you or attend a seminar. You possess everything you need. The key to understanding its power comes from building on who you already are. The difficulty comes in realizing this in a manner that makes sense to you, developing it, and then organizing a plan to help you achieve it.

Dr. Tony Daniel

The armies gathered for battle, each poised on opposite sides of the valley. Shouts from each side could be heard. The insults echoed through the valley. Israel's army was led by a proven man of war who had fought and conquered the Philistines many times. He and his army were arrayed for the battle. His warriors, proven in the past, were ready and waiting on the command. The Philistines, also ready for battle, had put their hope in a warrior, Goliath, who was more than nine feet tall. At times, this giant would come into the valley to challenge and intimidate the army of Israel. The sight of this man was fierce, and his speech would cause the men of Israel to quake with fear. The thousands of men didn't seem to bother them. It was the one man who was causing the problem. Saul, unlike in times past, was frozen with fear. He had no plan.

Jesse's sons were on the front line, observing these series of events. His youngest son, David, was caring for the family sheep herd. Jesse requested he take some bread and other provisions to his brothers. When he arrived at the scene, he heard Goliath yelling in the valley and his threats to the army of Israel. David, sensing the fear and confusion among members of the camp, observed that no one was willing to fight, something he had never seen. With confidence, he volunteered to fight Goliath. He was confident in the outcome and, therefore, was soon taken to Saul.

David, being very young, was thoroughly questioned by Saul and was immediately discounted for the role. Saul questioned David's ability based on what he saw and the present circumstances, a young and small youth, known only as a shepherd, requesting to fight against a giant fully clothed in battle garments, an experienced warrior. However, David was not discouraged and, knowing his value, began to explain his qualifications to Saul. He provided vivid details of past circumstances where he had been held accountable for the sheep and triumphantly fought much more dangerous opposition to protect them. Finally, Saul reluctantly gave in to David's request to go and fight against Goliath.

Although Saul thought he was sending David to his death, he reverted to his paradigm, a fighting warrior must look like one and possess the tools to fight. He clothed David in armor, including a bronze helmet and a sword, something that David had not been accustomed to wearing. David knew he could not wear the armor and fight, so he requested it all be removed.

After gathering stones in the brook, David approached Goliath. He placed one of the stones in his sling, aimed, and placed it in the one weakness of Goliath's armor, his forehead, killing him instantly and prevailing in the battle. Although you may have heard and read this story many times, there is an important part where focus is needed. Saul, relating to his paradigm and using it to protect David, was actually equipping his weakness. David, however, knew his strengths and knew what he could do if allowed to use them.

David understood a valuable concept. His level of value and performance was related to his strengths, not what others thought about him or what they saw. The same is true regarding your purpose. You will find it related to and among your strengths. These strengths are the best and most productive part of you and are innate. You'll be more confident and not afraid to confront problems that you know you can solve through them. Now this doesn't mean that you won't have to develop, hone, and practice them. When David confronted Goliath, it wasn't the first time he had used his sling.

This paradigm goes against what we are normally taught. In your work environment, a performance appraisal is an instrument used to measure your job performance during a specific period, normally a year. It measures performance based on job requirements and duties but does little to recognize and build your strengths. A low score often results in the formation of a professional develop plan (PDP) to address those areas of deficiency. However, the problem goes much deeper. What is being measured is a performance action, not necessarily a weakness. So the PDP addresses the result, not the problem. It is prepared with specific actions geared to prevent the weaknesses from creating organizational issues. It serves little purpose to address your strengths, help you develop them, and utilize them to create value for the organization. Based on your score, managers require you to attend training for deficient areas. However, most training programs are focused on correcting these weaknesses rather than identifying and developing strengths.

We often get so busy trying to correct our weaknesses that we forget about developing our strengths. However, many leaders and managers lack the understanding of this concept. The importance of focusing on strengths can be viewed from the scale below.

Succeeding on Purpose

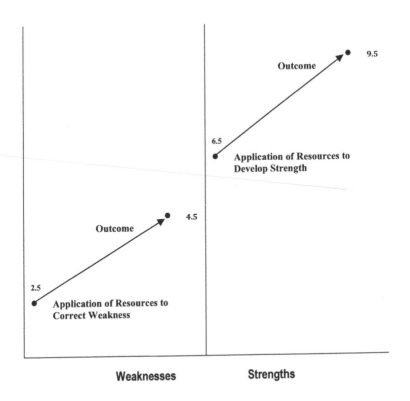

The chart indicates how your weaknesses and strengths react to resources when applied. These resources can include many different things, such as training, workshops, developmental assignments, job enlargement, books, and so on. To begin, look at where weaknesses and strengths begin on the chart. Even without resources applied, your strengths are above average. Next, look at the result when resources are applied to your weaknesses. Although they improve, the benefit will be minimal. In the chart, the weakness is still below average. Turning a weakness into a strength is almost impossible. David could have worn the armor of Saul for a time to help him adjust how to move and fight in it. However, he knew that applying his strengths would be much more effective. Now, look at the beginning point of your strengths. Its placement on the chart is already above average. This is the best part of you, and when resources are applied, the strengths move more effectively. The key point is that resources were applied to each. As a manager, which group would you rather have in your organization?

This doesn't mean that you should minimize the importance of managing your weaknesses. Of course, doing so helps you avoid major issues in your journey, but working to strengthen them is a less effective use of valuable resources. You can find countless books, videos, training materials, and tips to help you improve your weaknesses. However, when the focus is on improving weaknesses, the onset of many other problems occurs, such as stress, poor performance, health issues, and relationships. In contrast, how much more effective would you be if you could find resources dedicated to your strengths? Psychologist Donald Clifton, in a forty-year longitudinal study of more than ten million people worldwide, found only one-third indicated they had the opportunity to do what they do best each day. The study also indicated that those who do have such an opportunity were six times more likely to be engaged in their jobs and more than three times more likely to report having an excellent quality of life in general.[1]

Many leaders make the fatal mistake of attempting to be many things to a lot of people. Those with this flaw spend time trying to be great at everything but rarely exceed at anything. It's human nature to reach beyond one's natural strengths when wanting to do something great and worthwhile. However, success comes when you make the most of your natural ability rather than trying to do or be something or someone for which you were not designed. Effective leaders understand their strengths, the relationship between those strengths and their purpose, and that the combination can help them attain peak performance in all areas of life. They also have a good understanding of their weaknesses and surround themselves with people whose strengths fill the gaps. No leader has astounding strengths in all areas.

Dr. Ben Carson, retired neurosurgeon and the secretary of Housing and Urban Development in the Trump administration, understood the relationship between the use of individual strengths and positive outcomes. He used this concept often and applied it to complex surgical procedures. He stated, "I think one of the keys to leadership is recognizing that everybody has gifts and talents. A good leader will learn how to harness those gifts toward the same goal. Take the Siamese twin operations—when we gather these big teams, it's not because we want a lot of people. It's because this person is particularly good at this and that person is particularly good at that. You could get one person to do both, but why do that if somebody else is so much better at it?"[2] Dr. Carson had a clear knowledge of the value he brought to the operating room. But he also knew that others had more value than he in certain areas. Therefore, he had no problem utilizing other surgeons and medical personnel based on those strengths.

Most individuals have one or two strengths that set them

apart. Other characteristics are known as complementors that provide aid to the main set of strengths. Recognizing, pursuing, strengthening, and executing them is a key component of finding and living your purpose. To fulfill your destiny, you must have a clear understanding of your strengths and how to effectively apply them. Garnering resources and creating strategies to develop them is a critical component of growth potential.

Finding Your Strengths

You've learned that you already possess all you need to locate your purpose. You have been given certain talents, which are programmed in your DNA. You have specific attributes that outline your ability to excel in certain areas and situations. However, one major problem is that most people are unaware, or never take the time to learn and develop the awareness of their strengths. Peter Drucker, management expert, stated, "Most people think they know what they are good at. They are usually wrong ... and yet, a person can perform only from strengths."

As a consultant, I have often asked managers and leaders the question, "What are your top five strengths?" Most immediately refer to performance attributes, outcomes, and accomplishments. During the discussion, what I like to call a *teaching moment*, I relate that those are the results of strengths, not the strengths themselves. I have often observed a look of reflection and puzzlement as they reply, "I never really thought about it that way." Remember the story of David? He understood that his level of performance was directly related to his knowledge of his strengths and could, therefore, predict the outcome. Had he not had confidence in the ability of his strengths, he would have never opened his mouth. Having a clear understanding of your strengths provides you with the confidence to perform tasks competently. However, how do you determine your strengths and how to develop them? This is a maturational process that includes five different steps: self-evaluation, gathering the right tools, focusing on the key strengths, having a plan to develop them, and executing a strategy to use them. You will learn about each of these as you proceed through the chapters. But possessing the reality of who you are remains a precursor of purpose. There are a lot of ways to find out who you really are. However, they all should begin with some form of self-evaluation to help uncover the hidden layers.

Chapter 4

The Real You

Make the most of yourself, for that is all there is of you.
—Ralph Waldo Emerson, philosopher/writer

Carl Jung, psychologist, stated, "Who looks outside dreams; who looks inside, awakes." In the last chapter, I guided you toward a different type of thinking that turns your attention toward an awareness of your talents and strengths. As I share this concept with people, I see the wonder of connection, most of it from unaware associations, between their environment and their strengths. This association is a powerful component of effective action, yet most people never see it. The complexity of today's society makes it difficult to disengage long enough to think about your environment and your value to it, much less how and where to make the greatest impact. However, such an awareness affords you with the insight to put yourself in situations that provide you with the greatest potential for growth and positive outcomes.

Remember, you already possess all you need. You have an innate inventory available at your disposal. As you search this inventory, you'll find a common theme. The points are connected with a pattern that makes you who you are. You'll recollect certain environments and situations where you seemed most effective. In contrast, you'll also recollect situations where you were very uncomfortable and frustrated with no accomplishment. These patterns of events are telling you something. It's like sitting in front of the movie screen and seeing your life before you. The positives were situations related to your application of strengths; the negatives were situations that were more related to your weaknesses.

A deeper awareness provides you with a pivotal starting point. It is the foundation that allows you to understand, investigate, develop, and execute your strengths. It allows you to focus your energy on the most important parts of you. Wesley Clark, former NATO Supreme Allied Commander, stated, "I've never met an effective leader who wasn't aware of his talents and working to sharpen them." Dr. Donald Clifton, psychologist, was asked a short time before his death about his greatest discovery during thirty years of research on leadership. He replied, "A leader needs to know his strengths as a carpenter knows his tools, or as a physician knows her instruments at her disposal. What great leaders have in common is that each truly knows his or her strengths—and can call on the right strength at the right time. This explains why there is no definitive list of characteristics that describe all leaders."[1]

Process of Self-Evaluation

An accurate method of evaluating yourself is a critical component of personal growth. Many books have been written outlining the connection between your sense of self-evaluation and other outcomes, such as self-esteem, self-efficacy, emotional intelligence, social awareness, attitude, and many other areas. However, many researchers have linked one's self-confidence as a result of understanding one's value. In other words, self-evaluation is an ongoing process aimed at helping you gain a thorough awareness of the positive effect your strengths can have on your confidence. Higher perceptions of confidence are exhibited in higher-performance outcomes where lower perceptions of confidence can have negative effects, including physical. In 2008, following a twenty-five-year longitudinal study regarding the relationship between the awareness of one's strengths and the subsequent increase in self-confidence, Tim Judge and Charlice Hurst, University of Florida, studied self-evaluations from a cohort of 7,660 men and women who completed the survey in 1979, at the ages of fourteen to twenty-two years, and again in 2004. After comparing the results of the two surveys, they found that those who ranked higher in self-confidence in the 1979 survey experienced a higher increase in income than those who scored lower in self-confidence. Of the same cohort, those who scored lower in 1979 had experienced almost three times more health problems twenty-five years later. Those in the higher self-confidence group reported having fewer health problems in 2004 than they did twenty-five years before.[2]

It's also important to realize the direct impact self-confidence has on those around you. No one wants to follow someone who is insecure. Confidence breeds trust, loyalty, and a followership toward a higher purpose. It affects those in your inner circle, workplace, recreational activities, peer groups, and personal life. It is contagious and inspires others, something known as the *Pygmalion effect*. The term was derived from a story in Greek mythology about a sculptor from the island of Cyprus named Pygmalion who, after pouring a tremendous amount of passion into carving a statue of a woman, fell deeply in love with it. Aphrodite, the goddess of love, was so struck by Pygmalion's love for his creation that she descended to Earth and shot a magical arrow into the statue, which transformed it into a living, breathing woman named Galatea. When you are confident, your passion is contagious. Whether consciously or unconsciously, one's strengths can convey belief in and passion for others that can have life-changing effects.

David was confident, and he didn't have to tell others. He simply transferred that confidence into passion, which was observed by those around him. Four hundred men followed him when he had nothing to give. They believed in his vision, his influence, and his passion. History is full of individuals who, in the midst of trying times, displayed confidence in their abilities. The strength of knowing who you are and your value to your environment will keep you moving. Others will feel it, see it, and be willing to help you achieve it.

Tools for Assessment

You've learned that understanding your strengths is an important part of finding your purpose. You also learned that you have been giving all you need, the innate program exhibited by your talents and strengths. As Dr. Clifton related the importance of leaders having a clear understanding of their strengths, it becomes important to have a clear awareness of your personality traits. A leader is most effective when these characteristics are actively developed and engaged. Navigating the process of self-evaluation can be difficult and confusing. You will need help clarifying the information into an understandable format. It's important to reiterate that your behavior does not guide your thinking. Your thinking guides your behavior. Therefore, purpose must be addressed through a cognitive approach. From your talents come your strengths. Your talents are programmed through your DNA. Therefore, to locate your strengths, you must be clear about the structure of your DNA, primarily your personality. Sigmund Freud, psychologist, theorized that an individual's personality is fully developed by age five. Modern psychologists agree that although certain situational factors may have an influence on adaptation, your core personality remains stable throughout your life. A twenty-three-year longitudinal study of one thousand children in New Zealand revealed that a child's observable personality at age three showed remarkable similarity to his or her reported personality traits at age twenty-six.[3] The traits programmed into your personality provide the cognitive road map for your talents and, therefore, your strengths. So the use of cognitive tests to determine personality attributes can be an effective tool in this process.

As a management consultant, one of my major goals is to help organizational leaders and managers learn the importance of ensuring a precise person-to-job fit. This stresses the importance of the right person being placed in the right position based on a match between the strengths of the individual and the details of the position. All too often, a person is recruited for a position, especially on a team, without an evaluative process. The use of assessments provides leaders a more thorough analysis of individuals' strengths.

I use a variety of assessments to help organizational leaders push through the guesswork. These are primarily personality and behavior assessments that, through thousands of applications, have been refined to enhance the credibility, reliability, and validity of the results, thus bringing higher levels of confidence in the selection. There is a minimal cost for some assessments; however, many have free versions that can provide you with a starting point. I've compiled a short list that I use, but you should know that there are many at your disposal. Some provide more detail, but each is useful in gathering information. The more insight you have about your talents and strengths, the more understanding you'll have about where to focus your developmental strategies. This is not an endorsement for any of the assessments mentioned. It is for informational purposes to place an emphasis on the use of such assessments to help you in your journey.

Jung Typology Test

Carl G. Jung was a Swiss psychiatrist who studied under and later worked with Sigmund Freud. He developed a set of typologies, which was later expanded by Isabel Myers Briggs, a researcher and practitioner of Jung's theory. Through her work, the MBTI was created, which provides a more thorough component than the Jung Typology Test. The test indicates your personality preference in four dimensions, each having two different characteristics. The four preferences are represented in the table.

Section	**Overview**
Extraversion versus Introversion	General attitude or where you focus your attention, including your viewpoint on how you associate with others and where you direct your energy (external versus internal).
Sensing versus Intuition	Preference for how you perceive information, either from external or internal sources.
Thinking versus Feeling	Preference of how you make decisions and/or process information, either through rigid planning or through emotions.
Judging versus Perceiving	Preference for how you judge/deal with the world around you, either well planned or adaptable to alternative options.

Note: Assessment is free and found at http://www.humanmetrics.com/cgi-win/jtypes2.asp.

From sixteen different combinations, each having a distinct description of traits, the results of the test provide a four-letter personality type. The assessment is free and provides a good starting point. Here you can find descriptions of your designated personality type along with specifics regarding career choices, learning styles, and communication skills.[4]

HRPersonality

For a more comprehensive perspective, HRPersonality uses the Jung Typology to assess personality characteristics for use in the workplace through a Jung Typology Profiler for Workplace (JTPW) instrument.[5] Although primarily used for employment assessment purposes for the areas of candidate assessment, team building, leadership and staff development, counseling and coaching, and workplace effectiveness, it is an effective tool to help you identify your strengths and areas of application effectiveness. Most of the tips provided are specific to your personality assessment score.

The reports provide information about your most favorable behaviors, based on your personality profile, such as work style, problem-solving priorities, decision-making, and conflict resolution. You will also find suggestions for personal and career development that is specific to your profile, along with a quantified assessment of natural leadership. The report also provides insight into the best environment for you to leverage your natural talents and strengths. A major component of this assessment is personalized tips on developing your strengths and managing your weaknesses. There is a free trial for this assessment. However, there is a fee for continued use.

DiSC

The DiSC profile is different from the Jung Typology assessments. It is a behavioral profile that outlines a set of dominant and passive behaviors based on your compilation of responses to a survey instrument.[6] Each letter in the DiSC represents specific areas of behaviors. Each letter indicates an overall category, with each having more detailed characteristics.

- D—dominance
- i—influence
- C—conscientiousness
- S—steadiness

However, the key component in this assessment is that these behaviors are based on personality traits. In other words, as you read your profile and learn about the behaviors within your score, you should gain insight into your talents and strengths that highlight these behaviors. Also included is a description of the environment in which you, based on your score, desire and thrive. After completing the survey, you receive a thorough report that includes an overview of 15 classical profile patterns. As you read the descriptions of each section, examples will be provided that will clarify these points.

The profile is divided into four main sections labeled as Stages.

Section	Overview
Stage I	Devoted to your unique behaviors based on your responses. Includes a graph that highlights where you scored in each of the four areas, which provides a comprehensive view of how each one combines for a holistic profile.
Stage II	A comprehensive overview of the four dimensions and your personal profile within each.
Stage III	Overviews all fifteen classical profile patterns.
Stage IV	Provides the scoring and data analysis behind your report.

Note: Provided by *Your Life's Path* (John Wiley & Sons, Inc., 2003), www.yourlifespath.com.

No one score is better or worse than the other. The report shows your unique responses to your environment. It does, however, provide a lot of insight into your strengths and weaknesses. The key point is in recognizing your strengths and how they affect your behavior in a particular environment, which helps you realize your value. For example, attempting to use a strength in an environment not suitable for that strength would make you look inadequate when, in reality, you're in a situation for which you aren't suited. However, when placed in an environment that allows the strength to flourish, you would be more apt to thrive in the workplace and/or team.

In Stage II, the DiSC graph displays the intensity of each dimension from 1 to 28, which is divided into seven segments, each having a range of four scores. Behaviors, normally scored within a range of 1–7 that corresponds to your graph, are highlighted in each category. There is also a description of your behavioral characteristics within each highlighted area. You will normally see a pattern of characteristics among those in the areas.

The final area in Stage II provides a description for each dimension. Also provided is a list of environmental factors that you desire along with a section of factors to help you be most effective. Your score determines the importance of each dimension.

Based on your overall score on the profile assessment, Stage III provides you with a profile pattern. The description outlines your range of behaviors, which provides situational factors that benefit you in certain environments. Also provided are descriptions of work habits that are common to those in your profile range, along with insights that will help you apply these behaviors.

Stage IV provides you with the scoring and data analysis of your report. There are a lot of details in this section that can be beneficial to you. As you read the material in Stage IV, you will gain specific insights into your behavior patterns and situational factors that are specific to you.

The DiSC is an effective tool, when used properly. The results of the profile provide details that help you work backward to your strengths, providing valuable insight into where and how you would be most valuable. Strategically placing yourself into the suitable environment will highlight these strengths, thus making you more effective.

Harrison Assessments-Paradox Technology

This assessment is one of my favorites. I use it frequently when consulting with organizational leaders in developing leadership and management pipelines. The Harrison Assessment[7] utilizes paradox theory as a base for scoring. A paradox is a statement that is seemingly contradictory and yet perhaps true. According to paradox theory, a trait can be either constructive or destructive depending upon other complementary factors, such as environmental.

The Harrison is a behavioral assessment but is scored on a bipolar approach of measurement, which assumes an either/or relationship between traits by placing two related positive traits on either end of a scale. It measures these traits independently, thus providing a clear picture of more dominant traits. This becomes an important factor because the scoring mechanisms are based on a variety of positional factors, allowing you to customize the assessment for a specific category, which provides a more thorough analysis.

The assessment report consists of twelve paradoxes that relate to the workplace. It provides a graphical view of your tendencies related to each of the twelve paradoxes. Each pair is portrayed on an XY graph in order to depict the relationship between the paradoxical traits. Each graph is divided into quadrants, which depict the strengths and weakness of both traits. The information provided in each graph provides you with a clear visual of where your strengths and weaknesses lie. Descriptions of the scores provide you with insight into the placements on each graph.

The strength of this assessment is the use of the paradox theory, which provides a unique insight into yourself. Besides offering a window into aspects of yourself, of which you may only be partially aware, the HA System provides a guideline for balancing and developing you through specific plans for each of the traits. The site is very instructional, providing you with as little or as much information as you need to help you develop your strengths. Although the HA System is a behavioral assessment, you can use the results to work backward to your strengths.[7]

StrengthsFinder 2.0

Dr. Donald O. Clifton (1924–2003) was considered the Father of Strengths-Based Psychology by an American Psychological Presidential Commendation. His work, in association with Gallup, expanded more than forty years and was dedicated to finding *what was right with people*. The result was a list of thirty-four common talents. The Clifton StrengthsFinder assessment identifies your top five talents and provides a thorough explanation of each.

Following completion of the StrengthsFinder assessment, you will receive a *Strengths Insight and Action-Planning Guide* as a resource. The guide includes three sections. Each provides valuable insight into your strengths and how best to apply them. However, purchase of the book by Tom Rath, *StrengthsFinder 2.0*,[8] includes a sealed envelope in the back with a code. You will use the code on the site to access your assessment.

Section	Overview
Section I	Awareness—provides a brief description of each of the five strengths. Also provides a view of what makes you stand out from others along with questions that will help you increase your awareness of your talents.
Section II	Application—provides ten ideas for action for each of your top five themes. Questions are also provided to help you answer to help you apply your talents.
Section III	Achievement—provides steps to help you leverage your talents for achievement. Also provides examples of each of the top five themes, such as quotes from others who have scored as you.

Note: Taken from the results of my personal report. T. Rath, *StrengthsFinder 2.0* (New York, NY: Gallup Press, 2007), www.strengthsfinder.com.

Bringing It Together

There are numerous assessments that can help you find your talents and strengths. I've mentioned only a few. However, you need as much information as possible. All assessments are unique and approach the measurements in a variety of ways. Therefore, completing more than one will provide you with a more holistic view of your strengths. You will see patterns emerge among the different assessments that will provide you with vital information to help you with merging your strengths to the right environment. Be aware: you will learn not only about your strengths but your weaknesses as well. This too is enlightening and very important for your journey.

Having a thorough knowledge of this information is crucial to understanding the reasons for your successes and failures. Take the information, digest it, and use it for every part of your life. For example, if you're a big-picture visionary individual and view the world as abstract, you probably struggle with details. Therefore, for you to be successful, you must surround yourself with those who are detail oriented. If not, you will always be dreaming and never executing. If you're building a team for a specific project, you wouldn't choose all members like yourself. The team would generate some great ideas but would never get anything accomplished. Therefore, your strengths can add weight to your weaknesses. In his book *Relaunch: How to Stage an Organizational Comeback*, Dr. Mark Rutland discussed the importance of assessments when building a team and understanding the application of them in the organization. He discussed four different types of personality—Finders, Binders, Minders, and Grinders, which are descriptors of a lot of the personality measurements. He described the type of personality traits for each, and acting alone, they would be detrimental to the organization. However, when complementing one another, it makes the team stronger and much more efficient and effective.[9]

As mentioned, some assessments are free, and others have minimal fees. Stephen Covey related the investment in you as *sharpening the saw*.[10] This investment is critical to your future. Take the time and complete the worksheet to summarize the results of your assessments. Understanding the results provide you with a starting point. What patterns emerge? Write them down and use them going forward in your journey. The next step is committing to the process of putting those results into action.

Summary of Assessments

List the assessment that you completed and summarize the content. What did the assessment say about you? What are your strengths and weaknesses? In what type of environment(s) would you thrive?

Name of Assessment	Strengths	Weaknesses	Best-Suited Environment(s)	Summary

Chapter 5

Commit to the Cause

> We are made wise not by the recollection of our past, but by the responsibility of our future.
> —George Bernard Shaw, Irish playwright

I've introduced the concept of purpose and talked about the importance of finding and applying it to your life. You've learned that it is not some fairy tale that you just dream about but can never attain. You've learned that you have the tools fashioned as talents and strengths to pursue, develop, and live that purpose. However, this understanding, although important, is not enough. You must now harness all of the information you've gathered and begin developing an action plan. For without a solid plan, your purpose remains only a dream.

The foundation of this plan is laid with commitment. The level required is a full submission to the components needed to search it out. Such a commitment is a determined effort to give your resources to the cause. Mario Andretti, former race car driver, stated, "Desire is the key to motivation, but its determination and commitment to an unrelenting pursuit of your goal—a commitment to excellence—that will enable you to attain the success you seek." In other words, before desire can be channeled toward a purpose, there must be commitment.

Commitment is a cognitive process that, once chosen, is exhibited through a variety of behaviors, including garnering of resources, plans, and action. Vince Lombardi, former NFL coach of the Green Bay Packers, stated, "Once a man has made a commitment to a way of life, he puts the greatest strength in the world behind him. It's something we call heart power. Once a man has made this commitment, nothing will stop him short of success." Former president George W. Bush told the story about such a turning point in his life. Drinking alcohol had become a habitual behavior, which was affecting other parts of his life. In 1986, he and Laura, along with two other married friends, were turning forty. The couples decided to celebrate in Colorado Springs with family and friends. The former president woke up early and decided to go for his morning run, something he would regularly do to help him purge his system of the various poisons. During the run, the effects of his previous night's drinking became clear as he experienced the physical reminders. More importantly, the reality of the example he was providing for his family, his friends, and, most importantly, himself became very clear. He realized his drinking wasn't his problem; it was selfishness. Alcohol was becoming a priority, which was something he did not want for Laura and their daughters. By the time he got back to the hotel room, he had made up his mind to stop drinking. He told Laura that he would never have another drink. She had obviously heard this before and responded with a sly remark, "That's good, George." He admitted that he had talked about it before and done nothing. However, his next statement changed the course of his life" "What she didn't know was that this time I had changed on the inside—and that would enable me to change my behavior forever."[1]

Even though the future president had wanted to stop drinking on many occasions, it wasn't until he made the commitment in his mind that he would see the desired results. What was once a priority was eventually realized as a barrier. The commitment to remove that barrier allowed him to set in motion events that would eventually yield many positive outcomes and successes. The key point is that commitment must begin with your mind—a cognitive realization that some form of change must occur for you to move forward.

We have all known people who have made promises only to see them short-lived over a period of time. They had good intentions but never fully committed. How many times have you heard friends make New Year's resolutions, only to see them abandon them in a few days or weeks? Ken Blanchard, author and leadership expert, clarified the difference between the two mind-sets as interest versus commitment. Interest results in you doing something only when it's convenient. However, commitment to something results in you accepting no excuses, only results, and pouring yourself into whatever it takes to accomplish your task. George Bush had an epiphany and found a committed purpose to the change. Although there are many ways of determining commitment as a concept, it produces five specific outcomes.

Dr. Tony Daniel

Commitment Powers Motivation

Motivation is a drive to achieve a specific result. It begins as a cognitive concept, driven by the mind and witnessed through emotions and behavior. Factors of motivation can be viewed as priorities followed by some form of action. This is often a hit-and-miss that helps you clarify your correct road to purpose. Steve Jobs, cofounder of Apple, stated, "The only way to do great work is to love what you do. If you haven't found it yet, keep looking. Don't settle. As with all matters of the heart, you'll know when you find it."

One of the never-ending tasks of managers and leaders is the measurement of motivation among staff members. Creating and maintaining an environment that is conducive to higher motivation is critical to higher-performance outcomes. However, this is very difficult since every person is different. Some are motivated by extrinsic rewards, such as compensation and tangible items, while other are motivated by intrinsic rewards, such as the value of the work itself, including recognition and praise. Some are motivated, or demotivated, by the equity or inequity of the distribution of rewards or punishments, or procedural requirements. Understanding that there is not a one-fits-all program is critical to organizational health. Finding the right motivating factors for an individual can have positive effects on the outcomes. One reason is the level of commitment that rises when thinking patterns, the environment, motivation, and action work together.

The same process of motivation and action applies to you and your purpose. Motivation provides clarity, which channels away unnecessary thoughts, circumstances, and behaviors. This reciprocal relationship helps you see more clearly and enables you to effectively strip away the sludge of busywork and prioritize your energies toward positive outcomes associated with your purpose.

Commitment Creates Stability

Merriam-Webster Dictionary defines *stability* as the property of a body that causes it, when disturbed from a condition of equilibrium or steady motion, to develop forces or moments that restore the original condition. One of the clichés I use when consulting with organizational leaders, especially on the topic of strategy, is the reality that *there's a ditch on both sides of the road* should be built into every section of operations. Some may view stability as the centerline when, in reality, stability is anywhere between the ditches. Any variance can be corrected with little effort. Rigidity is a problem that creates barriers to opportunities. Just because you may have discovered your purpose and made a commitment to it doesn't mean you shouldn't be adaptable. However, keeping this metaphorical viewpoint of stability in mind, such commitment to the purpose should create boundaries of expectations.

Sandra Day O'Connor was born in El Paso, Texas, and grew up on a cattle ranch in Arizona. She attended Stanford University and, after obtaining her bachelor's degree, entered and graduated from the Stanford University School of Law. She struggled to find a job, due to opportunities for female lawyers in the early and mid-1950s being limited. She worked without pay for the county attorney of California's San Mateo region just to get her foot in the door, which helped her to soon become the deputy county attorney.

After working overseas, she returned to the US in 1958 and settled in Arizona, where she entered private practice. However, she returned to public service in the mid-1960s. She served in the Arizona State Senate for two full terms and was elected as a superior court judge in Maricopa County Superior Court. As a judge, she earned a reputation of being firm but fair.

In 1981, President Ronald Reagan nominated Judge O'Connor for a justice to the United Stated Supreme Court, where she received unanimous approval from the US Senate and served for twenty-four years. Her appointment broke new ground for women as she was sworn in as the first female justice. She was known as a moderate conservative who tended to vote in line with the Republican platform. However, although at times breaking from her ideology, she focused on the letter of law and always voted for what she believed was the intention of the US Constitution. Although variances occurred, due to interpretation, she argued her standard, "Commitment to the rule of law provides a basic assurance that people can know what to expect whether what they do is popular or unpopular at the time."[2]

This same standard of stability occurs when you commit to your purpose. You begin to filter information and measure its content. You recognize opportunities more clearly and expect results due to concentrated efforts. Variances may occur, but your commitment and the clarity it brings will keep you *between the ditches*.

Commitment Clarifies the Vision

On May 25, 1961, President John F. Kennedy spoke to a joint session of Congress. He presented his concerns regarding the US space program and the leaps made by the Soviets in recent years. He outlined the connection between a strong space exploration program and the fight for freedom and against tyranny. President Kennedy spoke of the benefits of such a program and cast forth a vision for Congress, NASA, and every American.

He asked Congress for a commitment of funds for the future of the American space program. Probably the most famous words of the entire speech rang for years and set in motion a frenzy of planning and action at NASA. "First, I believe that this nation should commit itself to achieving the goal, before this decade is out, of landing a man on the moon and returning him safely to the Earth." Along with this bold vision, the president laid out a list of associated goals with an aggressive space program, including a satellite system for worldwide weather observation.

President Kennedy's challenge to Congress set in motion plans for a coordinated effort among the scientific, technical, manpower, material and facilities, and research and development communities that would highlight the power of being committed to a purpose. Although President Kennedy would not live to see his vision come to fruition, Americans witnessed Neil Armstrong and Buzz Aldrin land and walk on the moon on July 20, 1969. Today, we enjoy the benefits of a well-defined set of weather diagnostics that has helped save countless number of lives through early detection of weather threats.

As you commit to your purpose, your vision of the outcomes become stronger. You have an end point reference and can now provide a set of strategic actions to accomplish the vision. When conflicts and adversity arise, the commitment remains strong and the vision clear. Distractions become easier to resolve, enabling you to press on. The action component of your purpose, in detail, is discussed later.

Commitment Provides a Continuous Measurement

Commitment, because it begins as a cognitive concept, can be difficult to measure. However, it has its relationship to performance outcomes at the individual and organizational levels. Social scientists and other researchers use a variety of survey instruments to identify variables that measure commitment among members of an organization. Results can then be tabulated, analyzed, and proposed as having an impact through inferences to a specific population. They can also be used to implement changes that enhance the work environment and, therefore, performance of the organization.

Truett Cathy and his brother Ben opened their first chicken sandwich restaurant, known as the Dwarf Grill, in 1946 in the Atlanta suburb of Hapeville. Mr. Cathy stated, "Starting the restaurant and pouring all of my worldly possessions plus everything Ben and I could borrow into it taught me the full meaning of the word *commitment*."[3]

To chase their vision, they purchased a lot between two houses and, overcoming many obstacles, including rezoning, built the restaurant doing much of the manual labor themselves. Mr. Cathy rented a room from one of the neighbors so he could be at the restaurant most of the time. Although both were totally committed to financial success, neither were willing to abandon their principles and priorities. Being raised in a Christian home and attending church regularly, one visible way to relate this action was to close on Sunday. The restaurant was located on Highway 41 just South of Atlanta, Georgia, a federal highway, which was the main thoroughfare connecting Michigan to Florida (at this time, there was no interstate system) and near the Atlanta Airport, thus making the restaurant very visible and convenient for those traveling. Although a churchgoing crowd would have created a lot of revenue on Sundays, Truett and Ben stayed true to their commitment. In later years, when Chick-fil-A grew into a large corporation, Mr. Cathy was asked why he never opened on Sundays. He replied, "We should be about more than selling chicken. We should be a part of our customers' lives and the communities in which we serve."[4] This foundational principle is still present today throughout the company and is part of the core values of the organization. "Our founder, Truett Cathy, made the decision to close on Sundays in 1946 when he opened his first restaurant in Hapeville, Georgia.

Having worked seven days a week in restaurants open 24 hours, Truett saw the importance of closing on Sundays so that he and his employees could set aside one day to rest and worship if they chose—a practice we uphold today."[5]

Mr. Cathy structured the restaurant on three main principles, which are found in the company's vision statement. These principles—family, the customer, and employees—drive operations and remain a testament to the commitment of Mr. Cathy's generosity.[6] Through his foundation of faith, along with his philosophy of business and commitment to his core values, Mr. Cathy created one of most sought-after employers in the US. *Business Insider Magazine* reported that in 2018, Chick-fil-A generated more annual revenue per unit, $4.4 billion, than any other fast-food chain in the US while being open only six days per week.[7] With only 2,100 restaurants nationwide, it is the eighth largest fast food chain in the US, with fifty consecutive years of growth.[8]

As part of his philosophy of life centered on family, Mr. Cathy was also heavily involved with helping underprivileged children. As part of the foundation, Chick-fil-A owns and operates numerous group homes that serve abused and neglected children. These children are under the supervision of hired group home parents, paid by the company, where they teach a variety of life skills. The foundation also provides college tuition assistance and work experience throughout local restaurants. Although not a revenue producer for Chick-fil-A, the work these homes provide is part of Mr. Cathy's vision and his commitment, as found in the vision statement and core values. When asked to what he contributed his success, Mr. Cathy stated, "The key to our success, I'm convinced, was our commitment."[9] He drew this conclusion from the consistency of the data, adherence to the core values, the work being performed, and the outcomes produced.

It becomes easy to fall prey to the pressures associated with life. The results from the measurements are a constant reminder that you have not become sidetracked. As you initiate the actions to fulfill your purpose, measuring along the way will keep you focused. If you fail to see the results or seem to lose the feeling you had when beginning, it may be a signal that you need to redirect your efforts and evaluate your position. Just as organizational leaders must continually align performance outcomes with the mission of the organization, an examination of the key components of your personal mission statement and actions would be a starting point. You may realize the need for adjustments.

Commitment Sustains You during Tough Times

Although adversity will be discussed in a later chapter, it is worth mentioning here with the topic of commitment. I've discussed the issue of conflict when searching for your purpose. Working the process will peel back layers of yourself that will be uncomfortable for you to realistically face. Fighting through feelings of rejection from others who want to keep you in that box can become daunting. If not careful, such feelings can guide your thinking away from your commitment to the cause.

Andrew Young, a civil rights activist who worked on the team with Dr. Martin Luther King in the civil rights movement of the 1960s, wrote about the turbulent times in their quest for equality. While in Birmingham, Alabama, wearied from the work toward the goal set forth and the abuse the team had suffered, he reiterated the goal through the guidance of commitment, "We didn't view success as defeating opponents, rather we wanted to make Birmingham a better place to live and work, and we were able to achieve that because of the tremendous spiritual power of Birmingham's black citizens and their willingness to forgive in the face of unspeakable provocations."[10]

Dr. King and his team, along with the citizens that joined the fight for equality, suffered severe abuse. They experienced physical beatings, psychological belittlement, dousing with water cannons, attacks by police dogs (while the officers looked on), being spit upon, and jail detention while maintaining peaceful marches. Yet the resolve of commitment to the cause never wavered. Dr. King and his team continued to clearly speak of the expected outcome and their commitment to the cause.

As you walk this journey of purpose, you will experience setbacks. You will become frustrated at the pushback from others. You will face adversity, from within and without, and make mistakes. However, having a clear understanding of your purpose and the commitment to the outcomes will provide you with solace during these turbulent times. Committing to the cause will help you understand the reasons and see them as a necessary component of the end goal. Conflict will occur, and you will feel like giving up. It's at this time that you measure your strength and your level of commitment. It is at this point, a point of decision, you will determine your path.

Chapter 6

The Battle with Adversity

Hardships often prepare ordinary people for an extraordinary destiny.
—C. S. Lewis, British writer

As he went to bed on December 9, 1914, Thomas Edison, legendary inventor, had no idea about the struggles he would face before morning. After spending a lifetime thinking outside the box, seeing the world that existed only in his mind, and creating goods, processes, and services that would change life as it was known, he saw more than half his work destroyed in a fire at his West Orange, New Jersey, laboratory. The fire was so intense, eight fire departments rushed to the scene and attempted to extinguish the blaze. However, the inferno, being fueled by chemicals Edison used in his experiments, was too powerful. In the end, more than ten buildings were destroyed.

Edison's son, Charles, who was twenty-four years old at the time of the fire, related in a 1961 *Reader's Digest* article that as he approached his dad, who was standing there watching much of his life's work go up in flames, expecting him to be very upset, he found him stoic and calculating. Charles recalled that his dad turned to him and stated, "Go get your mother and all her friends. They'll never see a fire like this again." When Charles objected, not wanting to leave his father alone, Edison replied, "It's all right. We've just got rid of a lot of rubbish."[1]

Too many today have fallen into the trap of thinking everything will always be perfect and that adversity is something bad or that it comes because you haven't done something right. However, there are times that bad things happen to good people. You may have the best intentions, plan strategically, implement carefully, and then experience setbacks. But in times of adversity, you won't have a problem to deal with but a choice to make. While standing there watching his countless hours of research and work go up in flames, Edison was confronted with a choice. He could have wept, yelled in anger, entered a deep state of depression, or blamed someone else. Instead, he understood that adversity creates opportunities. As he told his son to enjoy what he was seeing and to gather the family and friends, Charles learned that adversity had not only built character but was exposing it.

Thomas Edison was grounded in his purpose. He was confident in his abilities and had a thorough knowledge of his value. He understood that what he was viewing was nothing beyond rebuilding. During an interview by a reporter of the *New York Times*,[2] Edison stated, "Although I am over 67 years old, I'll start all over again tomorrow. There's only one thing to do and that is to jump right in and rebuild." He had already informed his employees to report for work the next day as usual and assured them that no one would lose their jobs. Edison's loss was estimated to be between $5 and $7 million (more than

$30 million today). Only about one-third of the damage was insured. About three weeks later, after a loan from his friend, Henry Ford, the plant reopened. Employees worked extra hard and, through inspiring leadership from Edison, dedicated their efforts to turning adversity into triumph. They worked double shifts to produce more than ever. The following year, Edison's company, which once laid in ruins, reported over $10 million in revenue.

Oftentimes, many are busy trying to be all things to all people and take little time to think about the value they possess. They confuse being busy with being productive. Doing so dilutes the application of strengths to what we do best. Adversity can be used as a stepping-stone or a stumbling block of defeat. Edison chose the positive. He knew that what had gotten him to that level was nothing that could prevent him from returning. Lord Byron stated, "Adversity is the first path to truth." It will come, but how you respond will determine how you go forward. One of the major keys to living and exceeding with purpose is to keep moving forward on the journey, making the best of the detours and interruptions, turning adversity into advantage. President Ronald Reagan, upon visiting his family home in Dixon, Illinois, which was restored and designated by Congress as a national historic site, spoke of his childhood as being tough. His family struggled to survive, and Reagan described the time as when he learned the real riches of rags. He related that his family held on to their dreams. They knew the stars would come out after the storm.[3]

Perspective during the Storm

Everyone likes some level of stability. There are those who live on the edge, taking risks, and those who are more conservative. Those willing to take the risks understand that adversity becomes part of the equation. They understand that moving from your routine into a life of ambiguity will create conflict. Therefore, understanding that pursuing and living your purpose will create conflict, within and around you, is the first step of accepting and facing adversity. In order to move from one level to another, some form of change must occur. It happens throughout nature, in science, and with each of us. Life is a one-way street full of detours. No matter how many you take, none lead back. Accepting this perspective creates freedom, which allows you to realize the simplicity of life in a few things.

Such free thinking is paradoxical to what we are taught all our lives. From early childhood into adulthood, we are programmed to abide by rules and laws, many that make little sense, that keep us constrained to a think-in-the-box fashion. However, your purpose will position you against popular belief, practices, rituals, and ideas. Society, however, seeks to maintain the status quo. It is when someone such as a Walt Disney or Steve Jobs comes along, who accepts no boundaries or limits in creativity, that extraordinary ideas turn into high outcomes. It is self-evident that if we can't take the risk of saying or doing something wrong, our creativity goes right out the window. The essence of creativity is not the possession of some special talent; it is the ability to focus on what you do best, accentuate the positives, understand the negatives, implement ideas, and expect results.

When focused on your purpose, the perspective of adversity becomes as random as good luck. In a study of one hundred executives, Michael Lombardo and Morgan McCall, behavioral scientists at the Center for Creative Leadership, found that serendipity, the phenomenon of finding valuable or agreeable things not sought for, was the rule, not the exception and that executives' ascensions were anything but orderly. Key events included radical job changes and serious problems as well as lucky breaks. Problems cited included failures, demotions, missed promotions, overseas assignments, starting new businesses from scratch, corporate mergers, takeovers and shake-ups, and organization politics. They concluded that adversity is used as an instruction mechanism. Successful executives ask endless questions and surpass their less successful compatriots primarily because they learn more from all their experiences and learn early in their careers to be comfortable with ambiguity.[4] They also noted that a common theme among the executives, which provided the mechanisms for these characteristics, was their directed passion built on a solid understanding of their strengths and value.

Alfred Armand Montapert (author, 1906–1997) stressed the importance of perspective when he stated, "The majority sees the obstacles; the few see the objectives; history records the successes of the latter, while oblivion is the reward of the former." So the question is not, are unfair things going to happen, but how are you going to react to them? Circumstances are rulers of the weak but weapons of the wise. Your perspective about adversity guides your thoughts and, therefore, your reactions. A good example of this concept was told by a dad who was listening to his daughter complain how difficult her life had become. As he led her to the kitchen, he filled three pans with water and then turned up the heat, causing each to boil. To the first pan, he added carrots; to the second, eggs; and to the third, ground coffee. After the contents in each had cooked, he put their contents into separate bowls and asked his daughter to cut into the eggs and carrots and smell the coffee. "What does all this mean?" she asked impatiently. "Each food," he said, "teaches us something about facing adversity, as represented by the boiling water. The carrot went in hard but came out soft and weak. The eggs went in fragile but came out hardened. The coffee, however, changed the water to something better. Which will you be like as you face adversity?" he asked. "Will you give up, become hard, or transform adversity into triumph to make the world a better place? As the chef of your own life, what will you bring to the table?"

As gold is purified by fire, you can be purified by adversity. As a committed individual to your purpose, understand that adversity will come but is only temporary. It's not easy. If it was, anyone could do it. Focusing your perspective on the conflict of adversity as a catalyst for growth will yield positive results. History is full of examples of people who overcame strong obstacles from which they found unordinary strength. The difference between them and others is that they never let that adversity define them but used it to learn and grow.

Dr. Tony Daniel

A Process for New Sources

Charles Handy, Irish author and management thinker, stated, "It is one of the paradoxes of success, that the things and ways which got you there are seldom those things that keep you there." Success can breed complacency, which breeds stagnation. Rick Warren, pastor of Saddleback Church in Lake Forest, California, put it another way, "The greatest enemy of tomorrow's success is today's success." Adversity often signals the need for change. As humans, we feel uncomfortable confronting change. However, understanding that adversity is conflict, and nothing grows without it, the presence of adversity sets you in position for new sources and avenues for growth.

In 1928, two brothers owned an animation company in California. They had created a character named Oswald the Lucky Rabbit and had contracted with Universal Pictures to distribute the animated character. A variety of other character-based products had been produced, such as Oswald candy bars, stencil sets, and buttons. The cartoon character had become very successful. One of the brothers, Walt Disney, went to New York to ask his distributor, Charlie Mintz, for more money to make more Oswald cartoons. After a short lunch, Charlie informed Walt that there would be no more funding for Oswald. Disney knew the brothers' studio would be forced to close without the funding.

Charlie also informed Walt that his entire staff of animators had been offered positions and would be joining Universal in New York. This was a blow to Walt, since he had hired his staff and taught them everything they had learned about animation. Disney was devastated. He had dreamed about owning his own studio. He knew he would start again with Oswaldo and pursue his purpose and passion.

Charlie Mintz, seeming to read Disney's mind, explained the fine detail of Walt's contract: Universal Pictures, not the Disneys, owned the rights to Oswald. Going forward, Charlie Mintz would make all Oswald cartoons. Mintz then offered Disney a job. Walt thought about his options and his dreams. He looked at Mintz and turned him down. He walked out of the office and boarded a train for California.

Everything Walt Disney had dreamed of and worked for had been ripped away. He had been clear about his dreams and had worked very diligently to pursue them. At twenty-six years old, he wondered how he would start over. How would he gather the support and resources? Starting over, would he ever make an impact in the animation business as he had dreamed?

During the train ride back to California with his wife, Lillian, Walt opened his sketching pad and begin drawing. He first doodled to calm his nerves. However, as he continued, a character began to emerge—stick legs and arms, a round body with big eyes and ears. Lillian looked at the character and named it Mickey. Mickey Mouse was born!

Disney had always believed that he, through his ideas and hard work, could change the world in positive ways. He refused to listen to others when they told him it couldn't be done. By the late 1930s, Walt Disney's cartoon studio was the most successful in the country. He went on to make full-length animated cartoon movies and eventually branched into other types of films, including full-action.[5]

Had Disney accepted Mintz's offer, not only would he have been miserable, but the world may have never known about his talents, strengths, and contributions. He was confronted with a life-changing choice. He could have accepted the offer and probably would have experienced some level of success and enjoyed a stable income along with some notoriety. However, due to Disney's commitment to his dreams and purpose, he refused to allow adversity to stop him. Throughout his life, Walt Disney approached each day with the belief that his purpose was to change and shape the world through his talents by working to make his dreams come true. He summed it up in one statement, "If you can dream it, you can do it."[6] On that cold and dreary late-winter day in New York, Walt Disney was faced with a life-changing decision. Choosing one would squelch his dreams. Choosing the other, which was very vague at the time, would allow him to chase those dreams but would cost him years of effort and demand he start over. At that moment in time, Disney was thrust into a state of adversity, which most would not be willing to endure—a level that could be debilitating to a career and dreams.

However, Disney never allowed his circumstances to define his value or direct his dreams; he adapted and allowed adversity to create new sources of opportunity. Understanding that any success he had experienced thus far was the result of his traits and hard work, Disney, as did Edison, only needed to redirect and apply the same elsewhere. It was him and no one else that was responsible for his success.

One of the weaknesses of many is the need for stability. Some accept and thrive on ambiguity, but overall, most like some form of stability. Some are more agile than others. They have the capability to easily shift to changes in their surroundings. Agility is the ability to move with quick, easy grace, having a quick, resourceful character. We associate agility with physical movements, such as Fred Astaire and Ginger Rogers, who moved across the dance floor with ease as if sliding on ice, or Barry Sanders, who as a running back in the NFL could suddenly change directions, leaving defenders grasping at thin air. Such examples, although entertaining and exciting, are physical traits. Real life is often not so graceful. Your ability to adapt is a mental strength that is critical to understanding your present situation, especially when undesirable, then shifting direction and moving. Henry Moore, sculptor, stated, "One never knows what each day is going to bring. The important thing is to be open and ready for it." As you grow and become sensitive to change, you'll find this ability in the midst of turmoil, which often gives you not only strength but new direction.

A lack of agility locks you into specifics, causes rigidity, and prevents the recognition of new avenues. The importance of personality was discussed earlier. How you respond to adversity can often be based on your personality, which drives how you see the world. Having insight into why you think the way you do can help create a deeper understanding about your adaptive capacity. Agility allows you to set your goals in concrete and your plans in sand.

Refocusing on Goals

Although the process of effective goal setting will be discussed in the next chapter, it's important here when relating to adversity. There have been countless books written on the importance of setting and pursuing goals. As related throughout these chapters, purpose should direct action. Your destiny is an end result that is realized through the systematic application of your purpose. Stephen Covey, professor and author, related that an effective goal focuses primarily on results rather than activity. Yet this does not diminish the importance of the details of your goals, for they outline the activities that produce the results.

Adversity comes as a disruption to the pursuit, and it's easy to become distracted with issues that, although you think are important, cause you to lose sight of the end result. Although the end result is important, the steps to accomplishing it are realized through some form of goal structure. Goals not only provide structure but organize direction to your mission. Remember that effective goal setting changes one's focus from that which he is trying to avoid to what it is he wants to achieve.

Having a clear understanding about where you are along your journey is critical to your goal systems. Creating a system to regularly measure your activity provides you with accurate information to help you adjust your plans accordingly. Ram Charan and Larry Bossidy emphasized this point, "Objectives should be measured by end results—measurement must be by accomplishment, not just effort put into the task."[7] Objectives are set as action plans to help you accomplish your goals. Although you may have to adjust your objectives, your goals should remain stable, thus becoming the measurement. Planning in order to merely avoid disappointment causes goals to be set too low. Therefore, keep the desired results the main thing and plan accordingly.

Chapter 7

Executing the Plan

> Your commitment level is proven by the effort given.
> Knowing what to do and realizing its value has no effect
> and benefit for you or others without action.
> —Dr. Tony Daniel, author and speaker

Will Rogers, former entertainer and humorist, stated, "Even if you're on the right track, you'll get run over if you just sit there, cause these times, they are a 'changing'." Throughout the previous sections, you've been introduced to the concept of purpose, where you find it, and how to develop and refine it. However, all of these create only busywork unless you do something to put it all into action. Throughout the book of Proverbs, Solomon referred to the importance of action more than one hundred times. John Wooden, legendary basketball coach who led the UCLA Bruins to ten NCAA national championships in his last twelve years of coaching, stated, "Decisions and intentions are honorable, but are useless without action." Michael Forbes, publisher, also stated, "Thinking well is wise; planning well, wiser; doing well wisest and best of all."

An action-oriented mentality is critical to success. It requires a different type of thinking, one that is uncommon to the majority. Many believe that movement must be measured in great terms. However, understand that incremental movement is still movement. Resting and reflecting is also movement and just as important. Remember, your thinking controls your behavior. Unsuccessful people focus their thinking on survival. Average people focus their thinking on maintenance. However, successful people focus their thinking on progress, which is only attained through action.

Lifelong learner has been a buzz word for many years. It is even more necessary in today's society where change occurs at an astounding pace. The ability to obtain knowledge is a great feat. However, learning without action is debilitating not only to yourself but to others as well. The transfer of knowledge reduces the *paralysis of analysis* and allows you and others to benefit from what you learn. The world will never know what thoughts, ideas, plans, and purposes you may have had that could have produced superior outcomes, had only you acted on them. You'll always have doubters, those voices from the sidelines, that call out and remind you of every reason you cannot or should not do something. However, all you need is one reason why you should. Believe it, take the first step, and you'll be on your way. Once you move, the law of momentum will take over, and you'll find it much easier to continue.

One of the strongest feelings of discontent is regret. Your feelings of regret will be stronger because of what you didn't do than those things you did. Realizing how we wasted our gifts and opportunities can create debilitating stress. Everyone has a past and the regrets that come with it. It's a natural process to think about those things and what we could have done differently. However, spending time on such is futile. Focusing on the past is reactive and keeps you in the status quo. Being proactive unleashes your potential to take your knowledge, experience, and dreams and funnel them to the plan of living your purpose. Greg Anderson, author and founder of the American Wellness Project, stated, "Think *impossible* and dreams get discarded, projects get abandoned, and hope for wellness is torpedoed. But let someone yell, *it's possible*, and resources we hadn't been aware of come rushing in to assist us in our quest. I believe we are all potentially brilliant and creative—but only if we believe it, only if we have an attitude of positive expectancy toward our ideas, and only if we act on them."

Transforming your thinking and planning to action demands a set of key principles to which you must first commit and then activate. Mary Webb, English novelist, stated, "Saddle your dreams before you ride them." Dreams are great, but you must have an understanding of the process. The application of these principles must be intentional. Therefore, you must be strategic in formulating and then implementing your plan. It has nothing to do with luck. It is about beginning with the end in mind and creating a set of calculated actions that put you on your way toward accomplishing the outcomes. Your purpose is created twice—first mentally, then physically. Being able to recognize that a fork in the road is not a problem but an opportunity is critical to moving forward. You may choose wrong at times, but experience is a great teacher and never fatal. You simply learn and use the wisdom gained at the next fork-of-decision.

At times, shifting from learning to executing can be a difficult process. However, Mark Twain simplified the process by stating, "The secret to getting ahead is getting started. The secret to getting started is breaking your complex, overwhelming tasks into small manageable tasks, and then starting on the first one." But, before you can start, you must have an idea of where to begin. Once clear about your position, execute and follow up. So many people expect good things to happen yet never prepare and implement their plans. To act doesn't always mean you have all the answers; you just need to get started.

Forming Your Strategy

Strategy, a term primarily used in organizational management circles, is simply a set of interrelated actions that, when implemented, has the purpose of setting the organization apart from its competitors. In other words, a well-defined strategy should create a competitive advantage for the organization in the marketplace. Although this may seem really simple, it is a complex process.

The principle of strategic thinking can be used in personal ways to help you initiate calculated action that moves you through a series of steps to accomplish your mission. However, just as organizational leaders must be clear as to the steps of an organizational strategy, you must be clear about the usefulness of each step in your strategy. For example, pretend that you wish to visit the pier in Santa Monica, California. It is a beautiful place with a pristine view of the San Gabriel Mountains running the shoreline of the Pacific Coast Highway. This visit is not the strategy but the outcome of a variety of necessary steps that are realized through a process of decisions. Before the decisions can be made, there are many variables that must be considered. Consider, for example, the various ways you could reach the coastline. Each would depend on a variety of other factors, such as time, money, desire, location, and so on. No matter how you choose to get there, you must first have a clear understanding of your current position and the resources needed. It creates the baseline for a measurement of your progress. The same process is necessary for you to implement plans to put your strategy to work and experience any result.

Earlier, I introduced the importance of analysis. By now, you should realize the necessity of gaining a thorough understanding of who you are, where you are along the continuum, your talents and strengths, and in what environment you would flourish. All you need now is to develop a plan to get you there. Jack Welch, former CEO of General Electric, summed up the process in very simple, yet profound terms, "Strategy is first trying to understand where you sit in today's world. Not where you wish you were or where you hope you would be, but where you are. Then it's trying to understand where you want to be five years out. Finally, it's assessing the realistic changes of getting from there to there." Although Jack was talking about forming a strategy for organizations, the same process is relevant in your personal life.

Revisiting a point made earlier regarding your personal mission statement, every action step in your strategy must be a measurement of support for it. Each goal must be related to it, and every step should be working to fulfill some part of the statement, either the what, how, or why. So you must ask, "Is it related?" As you move to plan and develop your strategy, you are creating a form of measurement for each proposed step. Every minute spent in planning will save you two in execution.

The Power of Goal Setting

The first step in the process is to have a clear picture of your goals. Before the era of GPS, an atlas or map was used for directions. Deciding where you were going and assessing the best route was important before leaving. As a child, I watched my parents on many occasions study a map and mark the best route. The map was kept close during the trip, where they would view it often to make sure we were on the right path. If a detour was needed, my mom would view the map and chart the way around the area to lead us back to the route toward our destination. Goals provide you with such a road map. Without them, your map is like a blank sheet of paper. During a conversation between Alice and the Cheshire Cat in *Alice in Wonderland,* Alice asked the cat, "Would you tell me, please, which way I should go from here?" The Cheshire Cat replied, "That depends a great deal on where you want to get to." Alice then replied, "I don't much care." The Cheshire Cat calmly replied, "Then it doesn't much matter which way you go." Alice's next statement is true of a lot of people. She replied to the Cheshire Cat, "So long as I get somewhere," to which the Cheshire Cat replied, "Oh you're sure to do that, if only you walk long enough."[1]

As I travel and speak to groups, I find it fascinating that so many fail to realize the need to set goals, not understanding why they seem to never move forward. While discussing the power of setting goals and how to attain them, many look confused. I ask them, "How do you know what you're shooting for without identifying a target? How will you know that you've obtained your prize without knowing if you're in the correct race?" What I find is that most people see goal setting as an activity that is burdensome. Some see it as dreaming and unproductive or a waste of time. Others are consumed with the daily activities of jobs and other duties that crowd the time to think about their goals. However, for those who experience any level of success, goal setting is not just an activity; it is a mind-set and way of life. Goals aren't your destiny, but they are milestones to aid in your journey. Your goals shape the plan. The plan shapes the action. The action achieves the result, and the result brings your success.

The Goal-Oriented Paradigm

Earlier, you learned about the power of paradigms and how they guide your view and interpretation of the world. It's critical that the power of such paradigms be discussed again because, since they drive your thinking, they provide the basis of transitioning to having a goal-oriented mind-set. Andy Andrews, best-selling author, lost both parents within one month of each other. He was age seventeen at the time. Through several bad financial decisions, at age nineteen he found himself homeless and living under the pier in Gulf Shores, Alabama. Overwhelmed with feelings of hopelessness and despair, Andy, having nothing to lose, began to search for meaning. He began going to a local library, where he read more than two hundred books about individuals who overcame adversity and became successful. Through this process, he began to recognize certain thinking patterns about these individuals, which led to behavior patterns that contributed to their success. One overlying theme was that they all possessed a goal-setting mind-set.[2] None of them floated on the wind and hoped by chance that something good would happen. They were intentional and took control of the decisions that led to their success. From his reading and studying, Andy developed the *Seven Decisions* that became the driving force he used to transform his life. From this list, he wrote his first book, *The Traveler's Gift: Seven Decisions That Determine Personal Success*, which became a *New York Times* best seller. All of the decisions listed below are intentional. They are direct and clear.

- I am responsible; the buck stops here.
- I will seek wisdom; I will choose my friends with care.
- Discarding the pit of indecisiveness, I am a person of action.
- I am in control of me, a decisive heart.
- Today I will choose to be happy; I am the possessor of a grateful heart.
- I will greet this day with a forgiving spirit; I will forgive myself.
- I will persist without exception; I will find a way where there is no way.[3]

Before Andy could act, he had to come to the realization of where he was. As he began, his thinking changed, which directed his goal orientation, which changed his direction. He took control of his success and worked those goals each day with purpose, learning how he could change his current situation into something better.

Realizing that goal setting is much more than an activity, that it is a pursuit of something larger than you, changes your view of the world around you. These new paradigms become the foundation for the goal paradigm. This shift produces a drive and energy that will shield you from the pain experienced during the work. You see the world and act from a proactive, instead of reactive, perspective.

Goal Setting	Lack of Goal Setting
Proactive and looking for opportunities	Reactive and always trying to catch up
Person who is agile and ready for change	Person who is satisfied with mediocrity—no agility
Operating with balance and personal satisfaction	No clear direction and lack of personal satisfaction

Alexander Graham Bell, inventor and educator, emphasized the importance of goals: "What this power is I cannot say. All I know is that it exists, and it becomes available only when a man is in that state of mind in which he knows exactly what he wants and is fully determined not to quit until he finds it." When your focus is turned from simply establishing goals to realizing and digesting them, you're now ready to move forward.

Goal Development Is an Intentional Process

You can find as many books and articles on goal setting as you want. The possibilities for the angle of approach are endless. You can read about the famous acronyms used to set your goals and attend seminars and workshops dedicated to help you learn how to develop them. The topic has baffled historians, statesmen, philosophers, and leaders for thousands of years. Seneca, a philosopher and satirist (4 BC–AD 65), stated, "If a man knows not what harbor he seeks, any wind is the right wind." Therefore, goal setting is an intentional process with six key principles.

Realization of the Process

The first step in effective goal development is the realization that it is a process. They don't just appear. You must be intentional, and formulating effective goals is a strategic process. When working with leaders, I provide a short template to help them formulate their goal structure, which is a three-tier process: goal, objective, and tactical plan. Each goal will consist of two or three objectives (specific action items). Each objective will consist of two or three tactical plans. The key point is that the process must be intentional. Below is an example of an effective structure I use when helping individuals formulate goals. I've included a template at the end of this chapter to help you formulate your goal structure. Use the structure for as many goals as needed. An effective structure includes no more than three or four goals, three or four objectives for each goal, and a time-based component. Having more is usually difficult to work through and accomplish.

- Goal #1
  - Objective #1A
    - Tactical Plan #1A1
    - Tactical Plan #1A2
    - Tactical Plan #1A3
  - Objective #1B
    - Tactical Plan #1B1
    - Tactical Plan #1B2
    - Tactical Plan #1B3

Don't fall into the complacency of shortcuts. In reality, there are none. However, don't get stuck in the process. You must create a balance between understanding that setting goals is a process and overanalyzing the details of the process. Just like any type of process, there are many steps that are interdependent on others. Some areas will require you to take more time to accomplish a goal, while others may take less. Either way, understanding that this is a process will keep you from becoming impatient and frustrated. Prioritize, align, and implement.

Alignment with Your Mission Statement

Earlier, you learned the importance of forming a personal mission statement. It defines your *what, how,* and *why.* Since

Succeeding on Purpose

goals are steps that help you accomplish your mission, they must support at least one of these variables. Often, one goal may have several objectives, actions that help you accomplish the goal, but they must work together to support the fruition of your mission statement. If you can't connect your goal or objective to at least one of the components, then your alignment is out of balance. I recommend formulating goals to include all of the variables of your mission statement.

Be Clear

Fuzzy goals are as bad as no goals. Have you ever had your boss give you a task with vague instructions? You left confused as to what you should do, no idea where to begin, and no clear projected outcome? The same is true when you have a goal that you haven't fully defined. Be clear as to the proposed and accepted outcomes. What exactly does accomplishment of the goal resemble? If you've divided the goal into small objectives, be clear as to each one and the resources needed to accomplish it.

Time Based

There is an Italian proverb that states, "Between saying and doing, many a pair of shoes are worn out." Have you ever started something you felt worthwhile only to set it aside when something else came along that needed to be done? Later, you realized the original task never got accomplished. Setting a timeframe for each goal will establish a priority level. Project managers use this technique, usually a GANTT Chart, to help keep the project on track. As you prepare your goals, prioritize them, set a timeframe for each, and keep a log of time spent on each activity. Since many goals are maturational, having a time-based structure becomes even more important.

Baseline for Measurement

You can't control what you can't measure. So your goal must be measurable. This is the only way that you know whether or not you're on task. The measurement doesn't have to be quantifiable, but you should have some system to know where you are at any given time along the process. For example, during the process of writing this book, I outlined specific milestones that were linked with time and progress. I measured my progress toward each one, which provided me with a measurement of the difference of where I was versus where I should be. At these given intervals, if I was behind, I knew I had to make adjustments in one or more areas of my life, including my schedule.

Put Them in Writing

Verbally communicating your goals is noncommittal. Writing them down initiates a commitment to them. What you value, for that you make time. Doing so sets the other principles in motion. Years ago, I had an employee that worked for me. He entered the organization at an entry-level position. Through our conversations, I learned that his spouse was the VP of quality control for a major multinational corporation (MNC). Her salary was almost ten times more than his. He invited me to a New Year's Eve gathering, which my spouse and I accepted. Upon arriving, we entered the kitchen area, and I noticed a dry-erase board on the side of the refrigerator. Listed on the board was a set of goals for the coming year for him and his spouse. On the other side of the refrigerator was another dry-erase board with the names of their two children and a list of their goals. At the bottom of each board were the goals from the previous year. Each had a large checkmark beside it, signifying that the goal had been accomplished. I asked my employee about the boards. He stated that they place a high value on goal setting and teach their children the direct link between goals and success. He told me that they have celebrations throughout the year when each goal is accomplished. Dr. William Cohen, major general, USAF, ret., author of *The Stuff of Heroes*, included a passage from Victor Hansen, one of the authors of the best-selling Chicken Soup series, which read, "Write down your goals. Post them around your home and office where you can see them every day. As you achieve each one, don't just cross them off; Instead, write 'Victory.' Celebrating the successes makes you hungry for more."[4]

Leverage the Momentum

In the field of physics, momentum is referred to as a quantity of motion. The longer something stays in motion, the more momentum it creates. In other words, for something to create and maintain momentum, it has to first move and continue moving at the same or increased pace. From a standstill, it takes a few minutes for a train engine to get started but takes a lot longer to stop. It will not stop until the energy that created the movement is decreased or eliminated.

As you begin working on your goals, you may not experience a lot of immediate or rapid return. However, energy creates energy, and as you continue to move, the momentum you create will produce more results. They usually begin small but add up quite fast. Shaun King, American writer and civil rights activist, stated, "My theory on momentum is that the best way to produce it is through small, hard-fought victories that lead to bigger battles and bigger wins." In fact, you will experience three results from momentum.

Greater Experience

As you work your plan, you will find new ways to produce results. You will learn by doing and work through challenges. As you reflect on your successes, new ideas will emerge. Charles Givins, author, stated, "Success requires first expending ten units of effort to produce one unit of results. Your momentum will then produce ten units of results with each unit of effort." Understand, however, you should never view your accomplishments as a fixed or completed state. Relish your success. Enjoy the journey but remember that successful individuals continue to look for new challenges and opportunities. However, don't get sidetracked with the new ideas. Write them down and come back to them later.

Increased Confidence

Aimee Mullins was born with fibular hemimelia (missing fibula bones) in both legs. Both legs were amputated below the knee at the age of one year. She attended Georgetown University and competed in track and field events in the NCAA Division I and the 1996 Paralympics in Atlanta. Today, she is a model and highly recruited speaker throughout the US. She was included as one of the *Greatest Women of the 20th Century* in the Women's Museum in Dallas, Texas. Regarding momentum's power to self-confidence, she stated, "Belief in oneself is incredibly infectious. It generates momentum, the collective force of which far outweighs any kernel of self-doubt that may creep in." This momentum creates a patterned cycle of self-confidence to self-efficacy to self-confidence.

Inspires Passion in Others

During a talk to a group of leaders, Aimee related a story about a speech she made at a museum to three hundred children, ages six to eight. She related that she had brought a bag of prosthetic legs and laid them on a table for the children to see. As the teachers brought in the kids, she requested that she be allowed a few minutes to visit with the children by herself. As the kids came in, they were amazed at the legs, touching and feeling the prosthetics. Seeing their amazement, she asked them a question. "I woke up this morning, and I decided I wanted to jump over a house. If you could think of any animal, any superhero, any cartoon character, anything you can dream up right now, what kind of legs would you build me?" The children began to shout out a variety of animals and superheroes. She related a statement from a child that spoke loudly to her inner being. An eight-year-old asked her, "Why wouldn't you want to fly too?" Aimee stated that the entire room of kids yelled out, "Yeah!" She provided the impact of the statement: "And just like that, I went from being a woman that these kids would have been trained to see as disabled, to somebody with potential that their bodies didn't have yet, somebody that might be super-abled."[5] Accomplishment feeds enthusiasm and frees others to tap into their creative and innovative spirit. This momentum, which fuels passion, inspires others to reach deep within and view their world differently.

Celebrate Small Wins

The process of finding and putting your purpose into action is a grueling process. By now, you should have identified a series of steps in your strategy that put you on that path. However, this path is full of distractions and pitfalls that you will need to effectively navigate. Many people place too much weight on these obstacles and adapt their actions accordingly. This is both inefficient and ineffective. You'll spend most of your time trying to correct and adapt to obstacles instead of spending your efforts on eliminating distractions. The result will leave you feeling that you're not making any progress, which can lead to burnout. Of course, you must be adaptable, but your focus should be on results, not the obstacles. Burnout occurs when you fail to recognize and celebrate wins along your journey.

The buzz word *burnout* has been in organizational psychology circles for years. It emerges through a prolonged exposure to chronic interpersonal stressors and includes three key dimensions: overwhelming exhaustion, feelings of cynicism and detachment, and a sense of ineffectiveness and lack of accomplishment.[6] It's primarily used to discuss situational factors in the workplace. However, in recent years, it's gained traction toward describing issues in personal lives.

These dimensions are systemic and facilitated through a variety of experiences and actions. Just as you learned that momentum is the force created when something remains in motion, the same is true for negative experiences. Negative momentum is very powerful and difficult to overcome. The by-product is often disengagement, which is a state of low energy, weak involvement, and a sense of low self-efficacy. Therefore, the process of activities that create engagement can also create disengagement. The difference becomes how you navigate through the processes.

I've discussed the importance of breaking down the overall process into manageable steps. These steps, although connected to the destination, constitute the important parts of accomplishment. So, if the goal is to stay engaged, based on the definition, which maintains your momentum, then recognizing the wins in each step is critical. Conceiving a grand idea or broad picture is usually intuitive. Shaping that picture into a set of workable parts is analytical; it's a huge intellectual, emotional, and creative challenge.

Small wins reduce the burdensome task of grinding out the details. Recognizing them, however, begins with understanding your stages in the process, which should be related to the goals you've set. According to John Kotter, former professor at Harvard and author, there are three main characteristics in a good short-term win.

It's Visible
You should have no problem recognizing the win as progress toward the end result.

It's Unambiguous
The outcome should be clearly defined.

It's Related
You should be able to relate it to your overall process of defining and executing your purpose.[7]

You will experience disappointments and lose many friends who will not believe in your quest. The road will be lonely and full of bumps and potholes. There will be dead ends, things that just didn't work out, causing you to back up and refine your search. Just as pruning a tree is actually a benefit for growth and fruit bearing, these negative experiences are part of the process. It is during these times that you must remember your mission and concentrate on the wins instead of these negative circumstances. Creating small wins has four advantages.

Helps to Maintain Momentum

Rewarding accomplishments along the way breaks the process into smaller parts. This helps maintain the momentum and reduces fatigue. As discussed earlier, momentum is the constant power of motion for an object. As power companies install power boosters across their areas to ensure that signals of electricity remain high to all homes, small wins provide the same benefit by keeping momentum at work in your journey.

Provides a Measurement along the Continuum

You learned earlier that a key component of strategy is knowing where you are at any given time in the process. Celebrating the accomplishments creates a clear picture of where you are throughout your process. Since it divides your journey into sections, if something doesn't work at a later stage, you have a point to which you can return.

Sets the Stage for the Next Step

Once you reach one stage, you can now use it to build on the next. Remember, an important aspect of strategy is maturation. Therefore, moving to one stage is dependent on the accomplishment of a prior one. As you celebrate these small wins, you are now ready for the next step in your process.

Creates a Plateau for Rest and Reflection

Your process is a difficult journey. You're working hard to accomplish your mission. As you accomplish each step, it's important to stop, rest, and reflect on your work. Doing so provides you with insight into what you learned, which can be used to help you going forward. You can use your experiences to alter your plans for the next step. This insight keeps you adaptable and agile to changes.

Finding time to enjoy the journey is sometime difficult. You may have a personality that hinders you from relaxing. Understanding that this process is not going to be easy and often lonely is a key component of decreasing burnout while overcoming adversities. Create small wins and then celebrate them in some way. Doing so will refresh you for the next step in your journey.

Succeeding on Purpose

Goal-Setting Structure

Below is a goal-setting template that is useful in formulating and organizing your goals and objectives.

Goal #1: _____
Completion Date: _____
    Objective #1A: _____
    Date: _____
        Tactical Plan #1A1: _____
        Tactical Plan #1A2: _____
        Tactical Plan #1A3: _____
    Objective #1B: _____
    Date: _____
        Tactical Plan #1B1: _____
        Tactical Plan #1B2: _____
        Tactical Plan #1B3: _____

Goal #2: _____
Completion Date: _____
    Objective #2A: _____
    Date: _____
        Tactical Plan #2A1: _____
        Tactical Plan #2A2: _____
        Tactical Plan #2A3: _____
    Objective #2B: _____
    Date: _____
        Tactical Plan #2B1: _____
        Tactical Plan #2B2: _____
        Tactical Plan #2B3: _____

Dr. Tony Daniel

Goal #3: _____

Completion Date: _____

    Objective #3A: _____

    Date: _____

        Tactical Plan #3A1: _____

        Tactical Plan #3A2: _____

        Tactical Plan #3A3: _____

    Objective #3B: _____

    Date: _____

        Tactical Plan #3B1: _____

        Tactical Plan #3B2: _____

        Tactical Plan #3B3: _____

Chapter 8

Tearing Down the Walls

I've learned that I have the strength to change.
—Al Pacino as Michael Corleone in *The Godfather, Part II*

Ronald Reagan was sworn in as the president of the United States on January 20, 1981. He inherited an economy in shambles. A recession had begun. Unemployment was over 11 percent. Mortgage interest rates were over 12 percent and would continue to rise for the next five years. Due to failures in foreign policy, Iran was flexing its muscle in a new regime and was holding American hostages. The country's poor relationship with the US had created an oil crisis, which had resulted in a gasoline shortage. Long lines for fuel, along with rationing, was pushing the American people into high frustration and a need for change. As President Reagan began work on repairing the economy, a larger mission was at his core.

The Cold War between the United States and the Soviet Union was still strong, and President Reagan viewed Communism as a major threat to freedom and world peace. He referred to the Soviet Union as the *Evil Empire* and worked tirelessly for eight years to relieve the grip of Communism throughout the world and help Soviet citizens gain freedom. Incremental progress had been made through more than one summit with Mikhail Gorbachev, general secretary of the Soviet Union. Although Gorbachev had softened his stance, he was in a battle between the hardliners in the Soviet Union who sought to maintain control and the people who were suffering from the ill effects of Communistic policies.

One of the most brutal reminders of Soviet control was the Berlin Wall, which was built by Soviet troops in August 1961 to stop the mass exodus of German citizens from Soviet-controlled East Berlin to Allied-controlled West Germany. Overnight, families were torn apart, separated by the wall. Communication lines were cut from one side to the other. Railroad tracks were destroyed to eliminate shipping from the west to the east. The Wall had become a symbol of tyranny and the demonizing effect of Soviet control. Its mission was not to stop people from coming into East Germany but to prevent people from leaving. Chaos and control were now the main components of rule. Seeing it as an evil reminder of control and as a continuous push in his pursuit of eliminating the debilitating effects of Communism, President Reagan gave an iconic speech at the Brandenburg Gate in West Berlin on June 12, 1987. The most famous part of the speech was when he poised himself and spoke deliberately:

> There is one sign the Soviets can make that would be unmistakable, that would advance dramatically the cause of freedom and peace. General Secretary Gorbachev, if you seek peace, if you seek prosperity for the Soviet Union and

> Eastern Europe, if you seek liberalization: Come here to this gate! Mr. Gorbachev open this gate! Mr. Gorbachev tear down this wall!¹

It would be another two years before the Berlin Wall would come down, allowing new freedoms and the reunification of Germany as a whole state. President Reagan would see the wall, the sign of oppression, come down but not from the Oval Office. Although beyond his tenure as president, his fight for freedom and peace remains his legacy. As a reminder of this legacy, a large piece of the Berlin Wall is anchored on the grounds outside of the Ronald Reagan Presidential Library.

Walls create barriers with the purpose of providing some form of control. They regulate movement and the expansion of territory. Often regarded as security, they can become hinderances. They create divisions that separate one place from another. Setting boundaries restricts acquisition and growth, cutting off those on one side from the resources on the other. Their image means different things to different people. Although the image of the Berlin Wall was clear, we create walls, internal walls, that restrict the clarity of opportunities beyond our sight. Although we may not purposely create such barriers, they are formed through a variety of mechanisms. We allow paradigms, culture, values, beliefs, and our work to create them. If we are not aware of them, they can have a debilitating effect on the process of our professional growth.

I have come to realize that I am my own worst enemy. I am responsible for my failures and my wins. When things seem to be going wrong, I take a self-inventory and usually find that I've allowed myself to fall into a set of thinking patterns and behaviors that are blocking positive outcomes. These walls, most unintentional, make the journey of navigating life much more difficult. Moving forward demands some form of change, which is always difficult but necessary. The first step to tearing down a wall is the realization that there is one and it's robbing you of value. Tearing it down demands change, which for most is difficult to accept and manage.

The Change Paradigm

Tearing down walls creates new beginnings. It demands that you move from one constant to another, often without knowing or fully understanding what the future will hold. Earlier, I discussed the power of paradigms. Revisiting, a paradigm is a set of thinking processes used to interpret the world around you. This interpretation acts as a guiding mechanism for behavior. Nothing is more difficult than changing the way we think. According to George Bernard Shaw, Irish playwright, "Those who cannot change their minds cannot change anything." Creating a new paradigm where change is a constant mechanism of growth helps you become more aware about your relationship with your environment. Marsha Sinetor, writer and teacher, stated, "Change can either challenge or threaten us. Your beliefs either pave your way to success or block you." In fact, the most relentless enemy of achievement, personal growth, and success is the inflexibility to change. Dr.

Wayne Dyer, author, stated, "If you find yourself believing that you must always be the way you've always been, you are arguing against growth." Too many seek comfort. Staying where you are is comfortable. However, great things never come from comfort zones. You cannot grow and stay where you are. Throughout the search and execution of your purpose, you will be confronted with circumstances that will require one of two options: to step forward toward growth, which can often be ambiguous, or to step back into your safety zone. As you progress, you'll gain momentum, which will make the next decision easier. Eventually, you will realize that where you are is far from where you began. You'll look back to your beginning with a sense of wonder. You'll see those who are still there fighting for something better, without realizing the power is within them. Nelson Mandela exhibited this view when he stated, "There is nothing like returning to a place that remains unchanged to find the ways in which you yourself have altered."

This concept of a paradigm of change is nothing new for business. It is a part of the culture that drives behavior. In his book *Thriving on Chaos*, Tom Peters stated, "Excellent firms don't believe in excellence—only in constant improvement and constant change. That is, excellent firms of tomorrow will cherish impermanence—and thrive on chaos."[2] At the time of publication, the internet was yet to be created. There were no electronic communication outlets, such as email, cell phones, Skype, or other virtual devices. Beepers, fax machines, pay phones, telegraphs, and landlines were the norm. Yet Peters understood and stressed the importance of a culture of constant change. Change cannot be viewed as the enemy but must be embraced as a source for personal growth and learning.

Fifteen years later, the world had been introduced to new technology called the World Wide Web, which acted as a catalyst for new businesses and the rethinking of how businesses operate on a global scale. Seth Godin outlined the importance of this paradigm when he stated, "Change is now constant and the fundamental ideas we have built our companies and our careers upon are going out of style fast."[3] Changes in the external environment were creating the need for rapid internal changes. Many company leaders were slow to adapt. Many tried to manage change, never understanding that change was managing them. Today, in the world of business, winners change; losers don't. Change is the new normal, and those who embrace it as a paradigm will survive. Those who don't will fade away and be replaced by others who can provide services and products more efficiently, effectively, and more rapidly to the customer. Examples like Digital Electric Corporation, who failed to realize the future of desktop computers and servers, and Blockbuster, who failed to recognize the impact the internet and streaming would have on video viewing, are reminders that change is constant and must be incorporated into your personal inventory. You may say, "But this is a business principle." No, this is a personal principle. Organizations do not change. It's the ability of people to change that brings about results, both organizationally and personally.

Change Is a Process

Many books have been written on the theoretical concept of change. Those theories relate change as a process. However, throughout this process, in reality, change has only two major components. First is the cognitive process. You must realize a change is needed and adapt your thinking patterns toward a more productive result. Second is the behavioral process. Change is exhibited through behavior. Of course, if you're leading an organizational change effort, the processes are different, broken down into a variety of steps. However, creating a personal paradigm of change, although much simpler, involves these two components through the process. There are five concepts that are important as you create this paradigm, or belief pattern, of change.

Change Is Constant

Heraclitus, Greek philosopher, stated "There is nothing permanent except change." You can't pursue new way of thinking and hold on to the old. The world is changing at an astounding pace. Ways of doing things today will no longer be acceptable in the future. Understanding that we must continually adapt to a changing world provides us with the ability to meet new challenges vigorously instead of being crippled by them. If something has been done a certain way for two years, there is an 80 percent chance there is a better way of doing it. You must continually view your surroundings as temporary and accept change as a part of your life in the twenty-first century.

Dr. Tony Daniel

Change Demands Conflict

Physicists characterize the universe as a very violent environment that is subject to continuous change. Explosions from the collision of stars and galactic bodies, along with gases and the power of black holes, create a hostile environment. Yet these changes create an expansion of the stars, galaxies, planets, the Milky Way, and the universe. So growth comes out of the change from chaos to order. Change is uncomfortable and difficult. Some people accept it, but few like it. Change demands that you face the unknown. Learning new ways of doing something creates a conflict within you and, unless recognized and managed, can be debilitating to your attempt to move forward. Unmanaged conflict enhances the struggle between past and future. Charles Darwin, naturalist, stated, "It's not the strongest of the species that survive, not the most intelligent, but the one most responsive to change." As a child, you were taught that conflict was negative, something you should always avoid. However, to change, you must embrace the concept of conflict as a part of birthing new dimensions. Creative conflict is healthy. It creates an awareness of why you do certain things. This awareness provides you with freedom to expand, take risks, and create value.

Change Is an Investment

Change requires learning. Learning requires an investment in you. If you're not a lifelong learner, you're accepting mediocrity and the status quo. You can't wait for the right time or circumstances. Preparation is key to taking hold of opportunity. Abraham Lincoln understood the important of self-investment. Mainly self-educated with approximately only twelve months of formal education, he was a lifelong learner. After selling his part of ownership in a general store, he entered politics and ran for the Illinois State General Assembly. He lost the election with a finish of eighth out of thirteen candidates. Yet, understanding the important of the investment of learning, he stated, "I will prepare and perhaps my time will come." More than twenty-five years later, he was elected as the sixteenth president of the United States. If you have worked the process to find your purpose, you should now be seeking opportunities to learn about you, your talents, and situational factors that will enhance them in your surroundings.

Change Must Be Managed and Measured

This is the information phase of change. You can't control what you can't measure. Therefore, you should create some form of measurement to inform you where you are along the continuum. Change for the sake of change is never good. Understanding the purpose of change creates the foundational component of measurement. Just as a building contractor can see the results of the work when building a house, you should be seeing results from your efforts in moving from one level of change to another. Change yields growth and, therefore, progress. If you're not growing, reassess your steps in the process.

Dr. Tony Daniel

Change Is Maturational

Any form of growth is maturational. If you're not building, you're sitting still. Therefore, you must incorporate a plan that helps you build upon each step in the process. As you change and develop from one step to another, you learn new skills, which can be applied to a new level of required outcomes. In contrast, doing what you've always done and expecting a different result is unrealistic by nature. Mediocrity is the enemy of progress. Aldous Huxley, novelist and essayist, stated, "The rung of a ladder was never meant to rest upon, but only to hold a man's foot long enough to enable him to put the other somewhat higher." It's impossible to reach the top by staying on one rung. The more you stay in one place, the more disillusioned you become with your surroundings. You can't dig yourself out of a hole. Trying to do so only creates a deeper one. Don't expend your energy on things that are disconnected from your mission, for they have less chance of producing favorable results. Frank Herbert, writer, stated, "Without change, something sleeps inside us and seldom awakes." When you reach a plateau, consider it a milestone; celebrate it but realize it is not a destination. Then move on to the next part of your journey. A healthy appctite for change creates the dissatisfaction with the status quo and moves you to create and innovate.

Four Blocks to Execution

Executing your plan creates risk. There is no magic crystal ball to ensure success. If you've done your research, planned your steps, and gathered the resources, then you're ready to execute your plan. However, the fear of the unknown is continually present. You know no progress can occur without movement. You remain reactive, always trying to catch up while your dreams slip away. Recognizing that there are four main blocks to execution is a point of origin. Each is grounded in mediocrity and practiced from this reactive framework; it's important that you clearly understand the impact they have on your ability to tear down your walls and move forward.

Reactive	Proactive
Lack of vision	Clarity of vision and mission
Fear of failure	Understands success means failing
Sacred cows	Willing to break new ground
Lack of commitment	Commitment to purpose

Lack of Vision

Too many individuals lack vision and a clear picture of what success looks like to them. Distractions come, but a clear vision strengthens perspective. It's more than a goal; it's a reason to try again. When someone urged Thomas Edison to give up and asked him if he felt like a failure, he stated, "I haven't failed. I've just found ten thousand reasons why it didn't work." Vision clearly paints the big picture. The bigger picture leads to perseverance. Perseverance leads to longevity. Longevity provides more opportunities for success. Edison refused to visualize the penalties of failure. Instead, he focused on the rewards of success. Holding to a vision is difficult, especially when things don't seem to be going right. It requires you to see something that isn't there. When those around him were urging him to give up and painting mental images of his failure, Steve Jobs held to his vision of Macintosh computers and a new era of technology that didn't come to fruition until years later. He never gave up and adapted as necessary throughout the journey.

Fear of Failure

Years ago, I was a victim of this mentality. I was working hard to be a success but wasn't growing. To grow would have demanded that I take risks, something I wasn't willing to do because of a fear of failure. I lacked courage. However, I read a quote by Mark Twain, "Courage is resistance to fear, master of fear—not the absence of fear." The quote piqued my curiosity, and as I studied this concept, an amazing pattern became clear: those who had reached some level of success fought the same battle I was facing; they had to overcome fear and move forward. They had taken some form of risk throughout the process. I came to realize that this fear of failure was actually blocking my progress. It was fulfilling its purpose in my life. I was playing it safe and failing to realize that I was digressing. Another statement from Jack Canfield, writer and speaker, that spoke directly to my inner core was, "Fear keeps us from taking action, and if we don't act, we never get beyond where we are now." President Harry S. Truman stated, "The worst danger we face is the danger of being paralyzed by doubt and fears." This paralysis causes inaction, which limits your learning through experience and thus a vicious cycle.

The Cycle of Fear

Fear causes you to hold to the comfort of familiarity. Risking something for the unknown is difficult. In a conversation with an individual during a consulting session, I pushed him to expand, get out of his comfort zone, and take some calculated risks. With a serious look of concern on his face, he looked at me and said, "It's very risky, and I don't know what will happen," to which I replied, "Yes, but we do know what will happen if you don't. Don't let the fear of what could happen result in nothing happening." There can be no real freedom without the freedom to fail.

Fear causes paralysis, which keeps you within the boundaries of normalcy. You've seen individuals, maybe even yourself, who are natural procrastinators. It becomes opportunity's biggest foe and fertilizes the ground of difficulties. President John. F. Kennedy stated, "There are risks and costs to a program of action, but they are far less than the long-range risks and costs to comfortable inaction."

To learn, you must get out of the box—face something unfamiliar. Experience is a great teacher. It broadens your skill set and allows you to grow. However, inexperience is a death sentence to success. Peter Drucker, management expert and author, stated, "The better a man is, the more mistakes he will make, for the more, new things he will try. I would never promote someone to a top-level job who was not making mistakes, otherwise he is sure to be mediocre." Not doing so keeps you inexperienced, which manifests itself in an inability to face new challenges. I always created a culture of solutions-oriented thinking. I wanted decision-makers at all levels that thought in terms of solutions instead of problems. I would empower managers and employees to make decisions. Of course, there were limits to their decision-making authority. As the leader, there were many decisions that were my responsibility. However, once they realized that it was okay to think outside the box, the fear of mistakes was reduced. The creative exhibition of decision-making was enlightening. Did they always get it right? Of course not. However, the power to try was more liberating than the process itself.

Experience sets you apart from others. It helps you gain and refine the skills necessary for the next level in your life. Earlier, you learned the importance of refining your talents and strengths to fulfilling your purpose. Inexperience promotes the opposite, an inability to recognize situations where your talents and strengths are applicable. Therefore, the feelings of inability create a sense of low self-efficacy. The cycle then starts over until you do something to break it somewhere along the continuum.

Sacred Cows

As a management consultant, when asked to help organizational leaders solve issues in their organization, I always begin the process by implementing a phase of analysis, or diagnostics, which includes observing the interaction between people, their environment, and the processes. I observe interaction among people along with communication and networking systems between units. Patterns always emerge, and when I ask why they were doing it this way, I often hear the old cliché, "That's the way we've always done it," or "That's the way I was told to do it." Throughout my experience, nothing has been more challenging than attempting to change not only behavior but the basic assumptions of behavior. Earlier, you learned about the power that paradigms and habits play in your development. The traditions discussed here are those that are deeply ingrained to the point that one believes this is the only way something can be done correctly.

Edgar Schein, a leader in the study of organizational culture, referred to these rooted beliefs as *cultural artifacts*, which are deep-rooted beliefs possessed by people throughout varying groups and levels. These become so deeply rooted that they are hard to identify and even more difficult to address and change.[4] The dependence on these artifacts of traditions causes you to be reliant on the normalcy of your actions. Breaking new ground becomes difficult, not only to see the opportunities but also the need. You are oblivious to the changes around you and are either slow or fail to adapt until you finally recognize it's too late, or at least find yourself way behind.

A great example, although organizational, of the power of traditional frames of reference is the experience of Encyclopedia Britannica. In 1989, the company sold more than one hundred thousand copies of its multivolume encyclopedia and set a sales record of $627 million. Five years later, sales had plummeted by 53 percent. During this timeframe, leaders had failed to recognize the importance of the CD-ROM with its exciting graphics and speed of search. Microsoft, a major entry into the market with its Encarta CD-ROM, provided it for free with computer purchases. However, Britannica continued to push the sale of its encyclopedias at a price almost equal to that of a new computer. By the time leaders recognized the need for change, it was too late. The company didn't have the resources, both tangible and intangible, to compete in the market.[5]

Take a personal inventory of your deep assumptions about your life and your environment. Look for patterns of thinking and behavior that may keep you from moving forward. Keep a log of the activities and results, which you can then use to create new paradigms. Just because you've always done it a certain way doesn't mean it's right or the most efficient or effective way. It's like holding on to dial-up internet because it's cheaper than broadband. You may solve one problem, saving money, but create more problems.

Lack of Commitment

Earlier, you learned about the power of commitment to the cause. However, you must also commit to executing your thoughts and plans. Having a good idea is not enough. Executing the aspects of that plan to bring it to fruition is difficult. Committing to that execution is even harder. There will be adversity, and you will miss it at times. However, it's critical that you have a clear understanding of the commitment necessary to move forward. It would be a shame to get this far in recognizing and pursuing your purpose but failing to commit to the execution of the strategy to get you to the place of living it.

Dr. Tony Daniel

Redefining Habits

By nature, we are habitual creatures. We love balance and consistency and often disregard things that threaten it. However, as learning should be a lifelong journey, most of it is accomplished through doing. John Wooden, former basketball coach, stated, "The final law of learning is repetition. Absorbing and understanding something over and over again makes action instinctive." However, instinctiveness can also be the enemy of growth. Redundancy is a common problem for most people. A routine of getting up at a certain time, going to work, doing the same tasks day after day, coming home, preparing and eating supper, going to bed, only to do it again the next day, can create a mode of normalcy that is difficult to change. Charles Duhigg, author, related the power of the mind when he wrote, "Habits, scientists say, emerge because the brain is consistently looking of ways to save effort."[6] Habit can kill your purpose because when you stop thinking, you stop questioning and dreaming. Learning a habit is much easier than unlearning one. However, the choice is yours. You are in control of the habits. You create and feed them, as found in this anonymous writing:

> I am your constant companion. I am your greatest helper or your heaviest burden. I will push you on forward or drag you down to failure. I am completely at your command. Half the things you do, you can turn over to me and I will be able to do them quickly and correctly. I am easily managed. You must merely be firm with me. Show me exactly how you want

something done and after a few lessons, I will do it automatically. I am the servant of all men and the last of all failures as well. Those who are great, I have made them great. Those who are failures, I have made them failures. I am not a machine, though I work with all of the precision of a machine plus the intelligence of man. You may run me for profit or run me for pain. It makes no difference to me. Take me, train me, be firm with me and I will place the world at your feet. Be easy with me and I will destroy you. Who am I? I am HABIT.

Through years of studying the effectiveness of leaders, one common theme emerged. I found that those who were successful created and practiced the habits that those who failed weren't willing to do. Other than the fear of public speaking, individuals are most uncomfortable with change. Ovid, a Roman poet who wrote during the reign of Augustus Caesar, stated, "Nothing is stronger than habit."

You learned earlier that your thinking controls your behavior. Therefore, to change and create good habits, you must address the cognitive processes that form them. Many, however, fail to learn from faulty thinking patterns that trap them in destructive habits. Some may be those that create harmful situations, and others may be subtle that obstruct personal or professional growth. Either way, to recognize any form of success, you must evaluate your habits. Norman Vincent Peale, minister and author who popularized the concept of positive thinking, stated, "Our happiness depends on the habit of mind we cultivate. So practice happy thinking every day. Cultivate the merry heart, develop the happiness habit, and life will become a continual feast."

The focus on thinking processes as the foundation for change creates conflict. The mind is the battleground. It is a natural phenomenon during change. Positive results can be accomplished by practicing good and productive habits. In contrast, consistent bad habits breed inconsistent results. As you consistently develop good habits, and as you move forward, new habits will need to be developed. What got you there will not keep you there. Momentum is created, which breeds positive results and the short-term wins. Creating good habits that support your purpose lets you see it come to fruition.

Just as it's important to create good habits, it's critical to your success that you identify habits that are not consistent with your purpose. Do you see any evidence of these habits in the goals you've set? For example, have you set your goals to support your habits, or will you have to change your habits to accomplish your goals? Are new habits needed to accomplish your goals? What resources do your need to supply these new habits? If you've set your goals according to your mission statement, which is the foundation of your purpose, you should have no problem identifying them.

Apathy

Have you ever talked with someone who had really great ideas and detailed plans but never did anything to accomplish them? James O'Toole, leadership expert, stated, "Ninety-five percent of American managers today say the right thing. Five percent actually do it." I believe this is applicable to the majority of society. Most have big dreams and even talk about them a lot but never prepare a plan to accomplish them, let alone take some form of action. Apathy is defined as a lack of interest or concern. It is synonymous with complacency, which is being self-satisfied, especially when accompanied by actual dangers or deficiencies.

Apathy is in direct competition with action. Knowing what to do is great. Doing it is even better. The old saying *actions speak louder than words* is prevalent. People are always getting ready for something but never doing it. An old English proverb clarifies this, "One of these days means none of these days." Feeding the one-of-these-days mentality breeds the *paralysis by analysis* discussed earlier. Underestimating the importance of the details of a process can be detrimental to your overall success. However, focusing too much, or at least too long, on the details can hamper the implementation. Therefore, there must be a balance between learning, preparation, and action.

Learning

Peter Senge, founder of the Society for Organizational Learning (SoL) and lecturer at MIT, defined learning as a process of enhancing learners' capacity, individually and collectively, to produce results they truly want to produce.[7] Therefore, a key component of learning is agility. Today, change is occurring at an astounding pace. What you learn today may be obsolete, or at least deficient, tomorrow. Learning must be continuous and intentional. Being a lifelong learner will help you adapt to the changing environment to keep you current in the execution of your purpose.

Preparation

Preparation is more than learning. It is about being intentional toward your strengths. Preparation and planning are equal in the processes and details of your strategy. Always expect the best but prepare for the worst. Preparation will also help clarify the resources you may need for each step. In the end, proper planning helps you be more efficient. As a consultant, I help leaders realize deficiencies in their organizations. Part of this process is analyzing processes and their impact on the organization. One of the key components of this is helping them build contingencies into operations that will prepare them for emergencies to defend against disruptions that can be devastating to their business. Again, expecting the best but planning for the worst creates a mind-set of proactive arrangement of processes.

Action

There is no substitute for action. You can't sit in the bleachers and hope to score a touchdown. Movement toward your goals helps you understand the impact of your purpose. Movement helps provide a measurement. I'll state it again: you can't control what you can't measure. Remember, apathy is the direct enemy of action. Due to the fast-paced world of today, there is a strange simultaneous occurrence. While someone is thinking something can't be done, someone else is doing it.

Something in human nature tempts us to stay comfortable in our surroundings. We try to find a plateau, a resting place, where we have comfortable stress and adequate resources. We seek comfortable associations with people, without the intimidation of meeting new people and entering strange situations.

As you pursue your purpose, never get comfortable with the present. Rest and reflect, but never get to comfortable. Ralph Waldo Emerson stated, "There are many starters but few finishers. The great majority of men are bundles of beginnings." The outcomes of apathy may not be realized for years. You can't wait. A failure to launch sometimes creates situations that can take years to overcome. Before the Iraq invasion, President Bush sought counsel from many world leaders. During a meeting between the president and Prime Minister Siim Kallas of Estonia, a former Soviet Republic, the prime minister looked at President Bush and stated, "The failure of Western democracies to act in the face of dangers during the 1930s caused many countries in Europe to fall under dictatorships, which resulted in many losing their lives. Action is sometimes necessary."[8]

Understand that the bigger your dream is, the greater the gap between birth and fruition becomes. This knowledge will help you alleviate the danger of apathy. Don't wait for things to change. Don't be counted with those who are always about to live or waiting on more time. Don't wait until things settle down and there are no problems. This mental approach to your purpose will keep you locked in apathy. Today is the day for action. Learn, plan, and execute. Never sit still and wonder.

Epilogue

Moving Forward

> I firmly believe that any man's finest hour—his greatest fulfillment to all he holds dear—is that moment when he has worked his heart out in a good cause and lies exhausted on the field of battle—victorious.
> —Vince Lombardi, former NFL coach

Too many people today live in the past. They relish the stories of old, which, in itself, is not a bad thing. Reflection can be beneficial. However, when we stay in the past, we can't see the future. In other words, it's impossible to embrace a new vision when you're holding on to an old one. Using your past to build the vision provides you with valuable insight into what you should be doing, with whom you should be doing it, and why it's important.

Throughout this book, I've introduced you to information that will help lead you toward finding and living your purpose. Understanding that this is a long and difficult process that requires patience and perseverance is critical to the outcomes you seek. The key word here is *process*. Remaining vigilant and committed to the cause unleashes the potential within you. There is no magic power in having a dream. However, you can't just sit and wait on it to happen. You have to work for it. As

King Solomon stated, "A dream comes through much activity, and a fool's voice is known by his many words" (Ecclesiastes 5:3 NKJV).[1] Good things come to those who work for them. President Kennedy stated, "Things do not happen. Things are made to happen."

What makes the difference? You do! You are responsible for your time here and how you use it. No one else can fill your role. You have been given the unique talents and strengths to do just that and to do it at the highest level. The responsibility for building your journey to bring your purpose to fruition belongs to you and no one else. It is hard work and not for the faint of heart. Dr. John C. Maxwell, author and leadership expert, stated, "Success is achieved in inches not miles." Your destiny is built on the future but realized in the incremental pursuit of your purpose.

You've been provided the knowledge to begin. Continue in the vein of learning but keep the reality of action in front of you. Jim Rohn, American entrepreneur, author, and motivational speaker, stated, "Don't let your learning lead to knowledge. Let your learning lead to action." No one benefits from your knowledge unless it is transferred. There is a strong interdependence between the two. Anais Nin, French-Cuban-American essayist and novelist, believed that this interdependence is the foundation of progress. "Dreams pass into the reality of action. From action comes the dreams again; and this interdependence produces the highest form of living." Don't seek to be a person of success without ever realizing the meaning of success to you. Doing so will move you from a life of success to a life of significance. Your destiny is waiting. Your purpose will direct you; your passion will fuel you; your performance will secure you.

Succeed on purpose!

Notes

Chapter 1

1 Taken from *City Slickers* (1991), Castle Rock Entertainment / Face Productions / Nelson Entertainment, distributed by Columbia Pictures.

2 S. Covey, *The 7 Habits of Highly Effective People: Powerful Lessons in Personal Change* (New York, NY: Fireside, 1989).

3 V. E. Frankl, *Man's Search for Meaning*, rev. ed. (New York, NY: Washington Square Press, 1984), 165.

4 R. L. Leider, *The Power of Purpose: Creating Meaning in Your Life and Work* (San-Francisco, CA: Berrett-Koehler, 1997), 1.

5 Ibid

6 S. Covey, *The 8th Habit: From Effectiveness to Greatness* (New York, NY: Free Press, 2004), 5.

7 G. Benzoni, *History of the New World* (London: Hakluyt Society, 1857).

Chapter 2

1 Personal interview with Gretta Wilson.

2 Covey, *The 7 Habits of Highly Effective People: Powerful Lessons in Personal Change* (New York, NY: Fireside, 1989).

3 W. Bush, *Decision Points* (New York, NY: Crown Publishers, 2010).

Chapter 3

1   T. Rath, *Strengths Finder 2.0: From Gallup* (New York, NY: Gallup Press, 2007).

2   Quoted in Avery Comarow, "America's Best Leaders: Benjamin Carson, Surgeon and Children's Advocate," *U.S. News & World Report*, November 19, 2008, http://www.usnews.com/news/best-leaders/articles/2008/11/19/americas-best-leaders-benjamin-carson-surgion-and-childrens-advocate.

Chapter 4

1   T. Rath, *Strengths and Leadership: Great Leaders, Teams, and Why People Follow* (New York, NY: Gallup Press, 2008), 13.

2   T. D. Judge & C. Hurst (2008). "How the Rich (and Happy) Get Richer (and Happier): Relationship of Core Self-evaluations to Trajectories in Attaining Work Success," *Journal of Applied Psychology*, 93 (2008): 849-863.

3   A. Caspi, H. Harrington, B. Milne, J.W. Amell, R. F. Theodore, & T. E. Moffin, "Children's Behavioral Styles at Age 3 Are Linked to Their Adult Personality Traits at Age 26," *Journal of Personality*, 71 (2003): 495-514.

4   Find at www.humanmetrics.com/cgi-win/jtypes?.asp. There is not charge for this assessment. See also www.opp.com/en/tools/MBTI/MBTI-personality-Types.

5   Find at www.hrpersonality.com/assessments/personality-compatibility. There is a small fee but the site offers a free trial.

6   Find at www.thediscpersonalitytest.com. There are also many consulting sites that offer the assessment as a service.

7   Find at www.harrisonassessments.com. Some components are free of charge and others are fee related. There are consultants certified to provide the assessment. See www.drtonydaniel.com. Email: tony@drtonydaniel.com

8   T. Rath, *StrengthsFinder 2.0.* (New York, NY: Gallup Press, 2007).

9   M. Rutland, M., *Relaunch: How to Stage an Organizational Comeback* (Colorado Springs, CO: David Cook., 2013).

10 S. Covey, *The 7 Habits of Highly Effective People: Powerful Lessons in Personal Change* (New York, NY: Fireside, 1989).

Chapter 5

1   G. W. Bush, *Decision Points* (New York, NY: Crown Publishers 2010), 2.

2   Sandra Day O'Connor, biography (Retrieved from https://www.biography.com/people/sandra-day-oconnor-9426834

3   T. Cathy, *EAT MOR CHIKIN: Inspire More People: Doing Business the Chick-fil-A^{aw} Way* (Decatur, GA: Looking Glass Books, 2002), 38.

4   Chick-fil-A (2018). See https://www.chick-fil-a.com/About/Who-We-Are.

5   Ibid.

6   Chick-fil-A (2018). See https://www.chick-fil-a.com/About/History.

7   Business Insider Magazine (2018). See Businessinsider.com/why-chick-fil-a-is-so-successful-2017-8.

8   QSR Magazine (2018). See https://www.qsrmagazine.com/content/qsr50-2017-top-50-chart?sort=2016_us_average_sales_per_unit_thousands&dir=desc

9   Ibid (3). 42

10 A. Young, *An Easy Burden: The Civil Rights Movement and the Transformation of America* (Waco, TX: Baylor University Press, 2008), 277.

Chapter 6

1 Reader's Digest. Vol 78-Jn/Jun-1961.

2 New York Times, December 10, 1914.

3 B. Baier, *Three Days in Moscow: Ronald Reagan and the Fall of the Soviet Empire* (New York, NY: William Morrow, 2018).

4 M. W. McCall Jr., M. M. Lombardo, & A. M. Morrison, *The Lessons of Experience: How Successful Executives Develop on the Job* (New York, NY: The Free Press, 1988).

5 K. Greene & R. Greene, *The Man Behind the Magic: The Story of Walt Disney* (New York, NY: Viking Press., 1991).

6 B. Thomas, *Walt Disney: An American Original* (New York, NY: Hyperion., 1994)

7 L. Bossidy & R. Charan, *Execution: The Discipline of Getting Things done* (New York, NY: Crown Business, 2002).

Chapter 7

1 L. Carrol, *Alice's Adventure in Wonderland* (New York, NY: Macmillan., 1985).

2 A. Andrews, (2019). Taken from https://www.andyandrews.com/about-numbers/

3   A. Andrews, *The Traveler's Gift: Seven Decisions That Determine Personal Success* (Nashville, TN: Thomas Nelson, 2002).

4   W. A. Cohen, *The Stuff of Heroes: The Eight Universal Laws of Leadership*, (Marietta, GA: Longstreet, 2001).

5   A. Mullins, Feb/2009). "It's Not Fair Having 12 Pairs of Legs." *TED* (Long Beach, CA) Retrieved from https://www.youtube.com/watch?v=JQ0iMulicgg

6   C. Maslach & M. P. Leiter, "Understanding the Burnout Experience: Recent Research and its Implications for Psychiatry," *World Psychiatry* 15, no. 2 (2016); 103-111.

7   J. P. Kotter, *Leading Change* (Boston, MA: Harvard Business Press, 1996).

Chapter 8

1   B. Baier. *Three Days in Moscow: Ronald Reagan and the Fall of the Soviet Empire* (New York, NY: William Morrow/Harper Collins, 2018).

2   T. Peters, *Thriving on Chaos: Handbook for a Management Revolution* (New York, NY: Harper Collins, 1987).

3   S. Godin, *Survival is not Enough: Zooming, Evolution, and the Future of Your Company* (New York, NY: The Free Press., 2002).

4   E. H. Schein, *Organizational Culture and Leadership* (3rd ed.) (San Francisco, CA: Jossey-Bass, 2004).

5   J. E. Russo, & P. J. H. Shoemaker, *Winning Decisions: Getting it Right the First Time* (New York, NY: Currency/Doubleday, 2002).

6   C. Duhigg, *The Power of Habit: Why We Do What We Do in Life and Business* (New York, NY: Random House, 2012).

7   P. M. Senge, *The Fifth Discipline: The Art & Practice of Learning Organization* (New York, NY: Currency/Doubleday, 2006), 364.

8   G. W. Bush, *Decision Points* (New York, NY: Crown, 2010).

Epilogue

1   Ecclesiastes 5:3. *Scripture taken from the New King James Version. Copyright ã 1982 by Thomas Nelson, Inc.* Use by permission. All rights reserved.